Second Edition

Brief
Counseling
That Works

Brief Counseling That Works

Second Edition

A Solution-Focused Approach for School Counselors and Administrators

Gerald B. Sklare

A Joint Publication

CORWIN PRESS

AMERICAN SCHOOL COUNSELOR ASSOCIATION

CORWIN PRESS
A Sage Publications Company
Thousand Oaks, California

For information:

Corwin Press
A Sage Publications Company
2455 Teller Road
Thousand Oaks, California 91320
E-mail: order@corwinpress.com

Sage Publications Ltd.
1 Oliver's Yard
55 City Road
London EC1Y 1SP
United Kingdom

Sage Publications India Pvt. Ltd.
B-42, Panchsheel Enclave
Post Box 4109
New Delhi 110 017 India

Printed in the United States of America

Library of Congress Cataloging-in-Publication Data

Sklare, Gerald B.
Brief counseling that works: a solution-focused approach for school counselors and administrators / By Gerald B. Sklare — 2nd ed.
        p. cm.
Includes bibliographical references and index.
ISBN 1-4129-0457-9 (cloth) — ISBN 1-4129-0458-7 (pbk.)
    1. Educational counseling. 2. Solution-focused brief therapy.
3. Short-term counseling. I. Title.
LB1027.5.S4862 2005
371.4′6—dc22

                                                                2004013137

This book is printed on acid-free paper.

05   06   07   08   09   10   9   8   7   6   5   4   3   2

Acquisitions Editor:	Rachel Livsey
Editorial Assistant:	Phyllis Cappello
Production Editor:	Tracy Alpern
Copy Editor:	Brenda Weight
Proofreader:	Libby Larson
Typesetter:	C&M Digitals (P) Ltd.
Indexer:	Karen A. McKenzie
Cover Designer:	Anthony Paular

Contents

Preface

This book provides step-by-step instruction in how to use solution-focused brief counseling (SFBC) with elementary and secondary students. School counselors and administrators in particular will be able to relate to the typical student concerns presented. Teachers will also benefit, because each component of this approach can be used independently in a variety of situations and school settings. Other professionals—psychologists, social workers, pastoral counselors, licensed professional counselors, and drug counselors—who work with youth both in and out of the school environment will find the case studies especially relevant. The skill of conducting solution-talk discussions with students can help educators reduce arguments, improve relationships, and teach young people to assume responsibility and make better decisions in a supportive environment.

The book is intentionally short. Theory is discussed briefly; however, implementation is the main thrust. My approach is to lead the reader through the material one step at a time, including practice exercises at the end of the first four chapters and in Appendix A. I seek to provide the knowledge necessary to apply SFBC with children and youth. SFBC is an innovative approach ideally suited for schools because it overcomes many of the pitfalls that often impede school counselors. With caseloads often exceeding 500 students, counselors can devote little time to providing students with longer-term, traditional counseling. It is no wonder that school counselors face a dilemma—counselor education programs typically emphasize counseling theories that may be difficult to use under circumstances encountered in schools. Today more than ever, counselors need a focused approach suitable for a range of problems.

Solution-focused counseling is timely for other reasons as well. Recent trends in education are giving teachers and parents more control in staffing schools through site-based decision making. In the past, school counselors tended to respond to the school principal's needs and his or her perceptions of the counselor's role. As noted in Chapter 1, through restructuring, counselors now answer to an increased number of decision makers responsible for personnel decisions. If counselors don't distinguish themselves as providing programs that help youth remedy their academic, behavioral, and interpersonal difficulties, their positions may be in jeopardy. With these increased pressures for accountability, counselors need an approach that leads to rapid, observable change in students.

OVERVIEW OF THE CONTENTS

The book is based on the work of Steve deShazer (1985), who developed the SFBC approach. He discovered that by focusing on solutions rather than problems, clients were getting better faster than with traditional counseling modalities. Implicit in the model is the belief that clients are not always overcome by their problems. In fact, solutions are actually present even though they may be unrecognized. By rediscovering their resources, clients are encouraged to repeat past successes. As simple as this sounds, it represents a powerful, empowering dynamic that enables clients to quickly resolve the difficulties that brought them to counseling.

Chapter 1 presents the background and rationale for SFBC and its special relevance to school counseling. The chapter highlights the reasons SFBC techniques work well with students from various cultural backgrounds. A solution-focused mini experience guides you to explore the process personally in terms of your experience as school counselors and administrators.

Chapter 2 demonstrates how to prepare students for solution-based counseling and how to facilitate the initial goal-setting phase of the model. Step-by-step procedures prepare you to help students behaviorally identify what they will be doing to achieve their goals. In the section on the "miracle question," you learn how to help students explore their goals by painting a mental picture of what their lives would look like if they were problem free.

Chapter 3 describes how you can equip students to see instances of unrecognized success and exceptions to their difficulties. You learn how to encourage through "cheerleading" that reinforces even slightly successful steps students have used to better their situations. This chapter also covers scaling techniques students can use to assess their current status as well as progress toward their goals. The chapter concludes with detailed instructions for constructing a message—composed of compliments, a bridging statement, and tasks—that students receive at the end of each interview. A practice exercise gives you a chance to apply these steps in addressing a personal situation of your own.

Chapter 4 provides a transcript of one of my actual student cases so that you can see the entire process unfold as described in Chapters 2 and 3. The case includes prompts and a message to help you associate process and practice.

Chapter 5 covers the interventions you can employ in second and subsequent interviews with students. These interventions address the successes students have experienced since the previous meeting. The chapter also discusses the scaling interventions used during subsequent sessions to determine students' progress.

Chapter 6 addresses how you can help reluctant and mandated students become cooperative customers. This chapter also provides a step-by-step guide for using solution-focused methods for referred discipline cases.

Chapter 7 describes other applications of the solution-focused approach. It discusses the use of referral forms that help referring persons specify, behaviorally, what they expect from students as a result of counseling, as well as instances of success already experienced by the students. The chapter presents detailed examples of how to implement the solution-focused approach with puppets, guided imagery, small groups, and entire classes.

Appendix A contains an entire counseling session with prompts that provide you with an opportunity to practice making SFBC interventions and then compare your interventions to the ones I actually used in the session. Appendix B contains reproducible materials for use with solution-focused guided imagery.

WHAT'S NEW IN THIS EDITION

Over the 7 years since the first edition of this book was published, many exciting developments have made even clearer the value of staying focused on solutions—the second edition reflects these new ideas. In particular, the second edition highlights more applications of SFBC, presents new adaptations of solution-focused methods, provides new tools to help the practitioner, and gives more opportunities to practice the SFBC model.

In Chapter 6, this edition expands the discussion of ways school administrators can use SFBC as a positive approach to discipline that can help involuntary clients become customers in the process. The chapter includes tips on turning difficult and potentially confrontational situations into a means for students to identify and begin progress toward workable goals they can embrace. This edition also highlights the effectiveness of SFBC with diverse populations and discusses how the fundamental principles of SFBC make it so appropriate for students from different cultural backgrounds.

New adaptations of solution-focused methods include the use of puppets to work though the SFBC model with young children and a group technique suitable for a range of age groups, from older children through adults. This edition explains how puppets can serve as a useful intervention to help young elementary-aged students express themselves more effectively and gives case examples to show how the method can be applied. Another new adaptation—solution-focused guided imagery—shows promise in working with small and large groups of middle and high school students. Appendix B contains complete, detailed instructions as well as pages that can be enlarged and duplicated to create the booklet participants use in the solution-focused guided imagery group process.

This edition also features a new tool that can help you carry out the note-taking part of the model. These specially developed note sheets help you organize your notes for constructing the message you give the client at the end of the first and subsequent sessions of counseling. Reproducible copies of these note sheets are found in Chapters 4 and 5.

The opportunity to practice SFBC has been expanded in this edition of the book. Appendix A provides a transcript of an entire SFBC counseling session, to which prompts have been added to describe the intervention that should occur next. By using a sheet of paper to cover the response following each prompt, you have an opportunity to practice these interventions and then compare your response to the one actually used in the session.

WHO CAN USE THIS BOOK

This book is designed for school counselors, mental health professionals, school administrators, and counselor educators. The intent of this book is to present step-by-step instructions, coupled with case examples, to enable the reader to gain the skills needed to use the SFBC approach. The book will also serve as a quick reference guide if you feel you are "stuck" and need to refresh your knowledge of the SFBC process.

The fact that clients can see positive results in a short time provides a particularly important advantage to those of you who serve as school counselors and who often find you are responsible for serving large caseloads of students. Because this model focuses on solutions—rather than problems and their history—counseling in the school setting becomes brief and success comes quickly for students.

Mental health counselors, especially those of you working in mental health agencies, will also benefit from this book. It provides a framework for counseling clients—children, adolescents, and adults—in a way that is efficient, effective, and positive. By staying focused on clients' successes, rather than their problems, practitioners have reported that they leave at the end of the day feeling energized and hopeful.

After reading this book, those of you who are school administrators will have another tool to help you deal with the array of difficult situations you face. By focusing on the successes rather than the failures of the students referred to you, SFBC can turn a negative experience into a positive one for both you and the student.

Counselor educators have found the first edition of this book to be very popular and effective with their students. To date, more than 50 universities have adopted this text to educate their students in the SFBC method. Faculties in counseling programs have found this book to be a useful tool in their courses on theories and techniques and in counseling practicum. In a recent conversation, a professor told me that his school counseling students found the first edition of this book to be a very practical aid in preparing for the challenges that lie ahead for them as school counselors. His students also indicated that, compared to most of the required texts in mental health theory, they especially appreciated a book that highlighted applications and case examples in a school setting.

My hope is that this second edition will be even more useful in helping counselors and administrators effectively serve students and clients in a variety of settings.

Acknowledgments

Although my name appears on the cover, the completion of this book would not have been possible without the excellent training I have received in SFBC from John Walter. I cannot express enough gratitude for the significant contributions of Anne Domeck, who spent endless hours editing the pages and chapters of the manuscript for conciseness and clarity. Mona Cattan Lewis's interest in SFBC and dedication in transcribing case studies from videos were greatly appreciated. To the many participants of the workshops I have conducted, I am thankful for your enthusiasm and willingness to learn something new, especially Margaret Cavitt and Jed Turner, whose creative applications of solution-focused counseling to groups have been included in this book. I am grateful to Don Nims and Letitia Holland-Cundiff for contributing their application of puppetry with SFBC.

I am also thankful to the many students I have counseled using this approach, whose stories fill these pages with hope. They have made me a better counselor and educator, and my life has been inspired by their successes.

I am indebted most of all to my wife Anne, whose unconditional encouragement, empathy, and understanding made this edition of this book possible. I dedicate this book to you.

The contributions of the following reviewers are gratefully acknowledged:

Sam Gladding
President
American Counseling
    Association
Wake Forest University
Winston-Salem, NC

Russ Sabella
Past President
American School Counselor
    Association
Florida Gulf Coast University
Fort Myers, FL

Charles Thompson
University of Tennessee
Knoxville, TN

Mary Ann Sweet
Elementary School Counselor
Tomball Elementary
Tomball, TX

Pauline Schara
Principal, Retired
Santa Ana, CA

Sandy Magnuson
Associate Professor of
    Education
University of Northern
    Colorado
Greeley, CO

Nancy J. Melucci
Psychology Instructor
Long Beach City College
Long Beach, CA

Sue Godsey
Educator
Carl Junction High School
Joplin, MO

Patrick Akos
Assistant Professor
University of North Carolina
Chapel Hill, NC

Diane M. Holben
Director of Research, Planning,
    and Accountability
Allentown School District
Allentown, PA

Cynthia Knowles
Prevention Specialist
Consultant
Dansville, NY

About the Author

Gerald B. Sklare, EdD, LPCC (Licensed Professional Clinical Counselor), NCC (Nationally Certified Counselor), is a professor in the Department of Educational and Counseling Psychology at the University of Louisville in Kentucky. Both his master's degree and doctorate are in counselor education from Wayne State University in Detroit, Michigan. He has served as a teacher and counselor in elementary, junior high, and high schools; he has conducted workshops around the United States on SFBC; and he has practiced in school settings and in private practice using this approach.

CHAPTER ONE

Counseling in Schools: Problems and Solutions

Picture yourself right out of graduate school with a degree in school counseling, eager to demonstrate your effectiveness counseling kids at a school that has just hired you as their school counselor. You have wanted to be a school counselor for as long as you can remember.

A year passes and the picture has dimmed. You have become overwhelmed with your assigned responsibilities and find little time to counsel kids. When you make the time to counsel students, you find yourself feeling discouraged because you only have time to give students a few sessions, and this leaves you thinking, "What can I accomplish in a few sessions, so why bother?" Because your main motivation in becoming a school counselor was to counsel students, you become disillusioned and question your decision to enter the field.

Then a flicker of hope appears with the development of a counseling model that seems ideally suited for schools. This recent approach, called solution-focused brief counseling (SFBC), shows promise because it focuses on students' assets rather than their deficits, and only a few meetings are needed to help students get on track to resolving their issues. Because many of the steps in the SFBC process resemble techniques learned in other approaches, the model is relatively easy for you to master.

1

As you use this new approach to change the focus of counseling from problems to solutions, you begin to notice a change in the students you counsel. They seem more confident as they begin to recognize their strengths and resources that were previously unnoticed. You observe your students repeating their successes, which in turn beget other successes. Your sessions have a positive focus, leaving you and your students feeling upbeat. And because the students are doing all the work in your counseling meetings, you are going home after work energized and full of hope.

This sounds too good to be true; however, practicing SFBC in schools can help counselors deliver the kind of assistance that drew them to the profession, and it does brighten counselors' outlooks. As one elementary school counselor described, she no longer goes home depressed, thinking of all the unpleasant conditions her students face. Instead, she focuses on solutions and achieving goals. She noted, "I find myself more helpful to children more of the time and that makes me feel great knowing I'm doing what my title describes" (M. Cavitt, personal communication, February 15, 1996).

But why are so many school counselors feeling they can't deliver the help they were trained to give? Practicing school counselors commonly cite the lack of training in counseling strategies that can actually be applied given the realities of a school setting. Counselor education programs typically emphasize theoretical models of counseling that require longer-term therapy than school counselors have time to offer or that school districts want for their students. School counselors do not have the time or the training to provide such therapy. Long-term therapy implies in-depth assistance, which is beyond the scope of the school counselor's work. Although it is important for counselors to understand the theoretical underpinnings of psychoanalytic, psychodynamic, gestalt, behavioral, transactional analysis, rational emotive behavioral, Adlerian, and person-centered counseling, expecting school counselors to apply these models in a school setting is unrealistic.

Moreover, most counseling approaches used in counselor education programs focus on problems, thus implying that something is wrong with the client. This emphasis on deficits usually leads to an extensive and time-consuming exploration of problems, etiology, histories, and causes.

The media also contribute to the concept that those needing counseling have deficits and have failed in some aspect of their lives (Downing & Harrison, 1992). Television and newspaper ads that promote counseling accentuate people's inability to cope with everyday issues. Students exposed to these descriptions may see themselves as dysfunctional and believe that seeking help would further emphasize their negative attributes. With this perspective, students' reluctance to talk to counselors who stress their faults is understandable.

As a general rule, students who do see counselors are often referred by school personnel or parents. Rather than being "customers" of counseling, they come as visitors, usually honoring either a request or an ultimatum, and therefore do not commit themselves to the process. The real customers are the parents, teachers, administrators, or other adults who want the student changed. They own the problem. Counselors also can inadvertently be transformed into customers if they become more interested in change than do the children they serve (Kral, 1994). Youth who are referred to counselors may view counseling as really serving those who sent them, which results in resistance.

The difficulties of providing effective counseling are compounded by the expectations that immediate observable changes will occur. The managed-care trend reflects what is now demanded in the mental health arena. Counseling is to be effective and quick because mental health providers are required to limit the number of sessions for which they will be paid. Overburdened teachers, like managed-care providers, are frustrated with their students' behavior, academic problems, or both. They send youth to the counselor for a quick fix as if the counselor had a magic wand. Failure to rehabilitate an individual instantly can result in teachers losing confidence in counselors and the counseling process.

The more counselors are seen as failing to furnish essential counseling services and programs, the more school communities question counselors' value in schools. In the past, the school principal's needs and perceptions of the counselor's role influenced practices. Now, as a result of recent national trends to restructure schools, teachers and parents have a greater say in staffing local schools. Counselors now answer to an increasing number of decision makers responsible for personnel assignments. If counselors don't distinguish themselves as providing programs and services that help youth remedy their academic, behavioral, and interpersonal difficulties, their positions may be in jeopardy. Questioning the need for school counselors has already begun. Some school districts have contracted privately with psychologists, social workers, and local mental health agencies to provide counseling to students—counseling that was previously rendered by school counselors. Unless we school counselors respond to these changes, we will be relegated to being glorified clerks. Fortunately, school counselors now have an innovative counseling approach in solution-focused brief counseling (SFBC) that provides a solution to this predicament.

School administrators also often find themselves serving as counselors, as well, especially in schools with small enrollments and limited funds, where school counselors may not be available. Even in schools where counselors serve, in some situations the principal or assistant principal would benefit from using counseling methods with students. Extensive formal training in the field of counseling or psychology is not a prerequisite to implementing SFBC with students. The step-by-step methods described in this book can be implemented very effectively by administrators as well as counselors. Throughout the book, where the term "counselor" is used, the term "administrator" can be substituted. The SFBC approach described in this book will provide school administrators the skills necessary to implement a form of counseling that will be compatible with their role as administrators.

A NEW SOLUTION

Through the work of a number of innovative practitioners (Berg & Steiner, 2003; Berg & Miller, 1992; deShazer, 1985; O'Hanlon & Weiner-Davis, 1989; Selekman, 1997; Walter & Peller, 1992), a model of counseling has emerged that can have tremendous impact in school settings. Recently, this potential has been recognized in a number of articles that have appeared (Bruce, 1995; LaFountain, Garner, & Eliason, 1996; Murphy, 1994; Pelsma, 2000; Sklare, 2000; Thompson & Littrell, 1998). DeJong and Berg (1998) reported that 78% of children 12 years old and younger and 89% of children 13–18 years of age made progress toward their goals in counseling 7–9 months after SFBC.

In his early work with this approach to counseling, deShazer began to ask clients to notice what was better in their lives between sessions (deShazer & Molnar, 1964). Attention to problems that brought clients into counseling was not part of the assignment. It is remarkable that two thirds of his clients reported that things were better by their next session. Among the one third who did not indicate that things were better, half of these clients began to discover improvements that had first gone unnoticed.

It is interesting that many of the things that clients reported were better had nothing to do with the problem that had brought them into counseling in the first place. This was significant— solutions were occurring but often went unrecognized unless attention was redirected to highlight these successes. It also reflected a shift in emphasis from the traditional problem focus to a solution focus, where exploring the problem was minimized. For example, depressed clients are not always depressed, for there are times when depression is absent. Likewise, clients could identify times when the problems that brought them into counseling were absent.

Weiner-Davis, deShazer, and Gingerich (1987) concluded that perhaps positive change could take place even before the first counseling meeting. They began to ask those who called for appointments to notice between then and the time they came in for their first appointment what was better in their lives. Amazingly, they reported the same results that deShazer found with the task assigned for clients to accomplish between sessions. Clients concluded that perhaps the problems had been overemphasized. This finding led deShazer and his colleagues to conclude that focusing on solutions rather than problems would be far more effective, a major philosophical shift in the counseling field. Basically, they found that in counseling you tend to get more of whatever you talk about, whether positive or negative.

The movement to a solution focus removed the need for in-depth exploration of the historical antecedents of clients' problems. Taking the investigation of the causes and origins of problems out of the process dramatically shortens the time needed for counseling. When the focus is on solutions, counseling becomes brief. Moreover, as the focus changes to solutions, actions become of primary importance and insight is deemphasized. These outcomes make SFBC an effective model for working with children. Because insight is not necessary, this approach offers a good fit, for at some levels, youth do not have the cognitive skills essential to understand where they are and how they got there in the same way adults are able to grasp these concepts (Kral, 1994). Although identified as therapy by its founders, this approach is more appropriately considered counseling rather than therapy for several reasons (Littrell, Malia, Nichols, et al., 1992): The approach is relatively easy to master, it emphasizes problem solving and student-produced solutions, and assistance is provided in a school setting.

Solution-focused counselors found that by using their clients' words, counseling became easier for clients to comprehend. By using students' language, counseling was actually personalized to meet their needs. Students' abilities to communicate at a familiar level and to recognize that they are understood creates an ideal situation.

Another aspect of this method suits children well—the focus on using language that directs them to take positive actions. Children arrive at counselors' or administrators' doors most often because either they or the person referring them wants them to *stop* doing something (fighting, disrupting, talking, playing). Negative goals are very difficult to accomplish because, to imagine themselves not doing something, children must replace those thoughts with something concrete. Developmentally, children need examples of what they are to *start* doing. The solution focus presents children with what they *can* do.

SFBC also calls for clients to determine their outcome goals for counseling. Counseling focuses on clients' desires, not on the desires of the counselor or administrator. Clients are viewed as being their own experts—they know what is best for them. Having faith in clients' ability to identify their goals conveys confidence and respect, and when children are permitted to determine their own agenda for counseling, resistance diminishes. Giving up the role of the expert who knows what's best for students may be difficult for counselors and administrators. Effectiveness in using this method depends on the willingness to embrace this belief in the client's abilities; to allow clients to do all the work and assume all the responsibility; and to recognize that regardless of clients' past experiences or background, change for the better is possible.

Many of the skills associated with SFBC are shared with other counseling models in the field. Listening, responding with empathy, asking open-ended questions, supporting, reinforcing, identifying goals, and applying scaling methods are but a few of the techniques SFBC has in common with other mental health applications. Therefore, the transition to a solution-based approach becomes easier than you might imagine to adapt to your own style of practice.

As with any counseling model, this approach may not be effective with all students. Some may not want to be "fixed" because they may just want someone to listen to them. Students who have recently experienced a loss may not yet be ready to find solutions. Others may be cautious about your new approach and reject your assistance. Making students aware of your rationale for using this different approach with them may help alleviate their suspicion.

Keep in mind, SFBC is just another approach school counselors and administrators can use in addition to others found to be effective with students.

To personalize some of the concepts alluded to thus far, consider the following six questions:

1. If a miracle happened during the night while you were sleeping and the next day the problem of not having the time to counsel students were solved, what would be different?

2. What would you be doing that you weren't doing before?

3. Who other than you would see this difference in your behavior, and how would they respond to this difference in you?

4. When have some parts of this miracle already occurred, even during those times when you typically get sidetracked from counseling? What is different about these times?

5. On a scale of 0–10, with 0 being 100% dissatisfaction with your opportunity to counsel students and 10 representing the day after the miracle occurred and 100% satisfaction with the counseling you are providing, where would you place yourself on that scale now?

6. When you have moved up the scale just 10%, what will you be doing differently from what you are doing now?

These are the kinds of questions solution-focused counselors ask their clients. Answering these questions is the first step in personally beginning to comprehend the SFBC process. The central philosophy of SFBC provides the framework for the assumptions and concepts that guide this approach. Following a discussion of SFBC with diverse populations is a review of this philosophy, the assumptions, and the guiding concepts.

SFBC WITH DIVERSE POPULATIONS

Public schools have increasing numbers of students from culturally diverse backgrounds (Holcomb-McCoy, 2001). In fact, projections indicate that, by 2020, the majority of students in public schools will come from diverse cultural, ethnic, and/or racial backgrounds (Campbell, 1994). In some cases, cultural differences can be associated with issues related to trust. Some reports indicate that this may be particularly true for African American students (Biafora, Taylor, Warheit, Zimmerman, & Vega, 1993; Phelps, Taylor, & Gerard, 2001). In other cases, help with problems is traditionally sought from within the family, causing students to feel uncomfortable or unfamiliar with the idea of seeking help from a school counselor or administrator. This may be the case for children from a Latino background (Altarriba & Bauer, 1998). With children of Latino decent being the fastest growing population of school-aged children in the United States (Aviles, Guerrero, Horwarth, & Thomas, 1999), schools need to find ways to best serve these students.

The issues related to cultural differences have led administrators and counselors to seek a new understanding of how best to provide counseling services to students from a variety of cultural backgrounds. As an example of the attention being directed to these needs, an entire issue of the *Journal of Counseling and Development* (Robinson & Ginter, 1999) was devoted to the issue of diverse populations and the need for special care when counseling people from different cultural backgrounds.

Fortunately, many characteristics of the solution-focused approach make it an ideal counseling approach with diverse populations. SFBC sessions focus on clients' experiences within their own frames of reference—not the counselor's—and on discussion of solutions rather than problems. In addition, SFBC uses the client's terms and phrases rather than the counselor's, recognizes that clients are the best experts on themselves, and focuses on strengths rather than weaknesses. These aspects of the SFBC model help clients from diverse backgrounds overcome their resistance to counseling.

Support for SFBC with multicultural populations is beginning to surface. The first edition of this book has been translated into Japanese and Korean, and inquiries about translating the book into Chinese are being pursued. An e-mail message I received from a Japanese counselor indicated that the SFBC approach was more effective in working with Japanese clients than other counseling approaches she had used. DeJong and Berg (1998) found that 80% of African American clients and 82% of Latino clients (although the study had a small sample of Latino clients) compared to 71% of Caucasian clients of all ages either met their goals or made progress toward their goals as a result of SFBC. Many of the cases presented in this book were with African American students who came from poor neighborhoods. The success of these students in overcoming their difficulties was inspirational.

CENTRAL PHILOSOPHY

As with any counseling model, there are rules of thumb that reflect the core beliefs and lead to the most effective use for SFBC. DeShazer (1987, p. 59) and Berg and Miller (1992, p. 17) have proposed three basic rules for counselors using SFBC.

The first rule is the old saying, "If it ain't broke, don't fix it." Making an issue out of something that is not an issue for clients can cause difficulties in areas that were previously manageable to them. Counselors should focus on generating solutions, not additional concerns. Clients need to work on what they see as causing them difficulties; otherwise, the counselor's agenda becomes the focus of counseling. Following this rule means that counselors subscribe to the philosophy that clients—not the counselor—determine the goals for counseling.

Rule two is, "Once you know what works, do more of it." Recognizing those interventions that clients report as successful gives the counselor valuable information. Once successes are identified, counselors have clients replicate them. The temptation to become more elegant or try something different to move more quickly should be avoided. An assignment that has previously worked has an excellent chance of succeeding again.

In the big picture, clients tend to miss things that are working for them. They tend to direct attention instead to what is wrong and not working. Problems grow disproportionately in relation to the solutions, which generally go unnoticed. People tend to describe problems as always happening or goals as never being attained. These absolutes are not true 100% of the time. Students aren't always tardy for class, always disturbing the teacher, or never doing homework. There are instances when they are on time, are cooperating with the teacher, or are taking responsibility for doing their homework. These moments of success are frequently forgotten or generally unrecognized. Therefore, it is important for counselors to pay particular attention to indications of what works for each and every client so that these solutions can be replicated. In adhering to this rule, counselors commit to the belief that all people have been successful in overcoming their problems at various times in their lives. They have the ability to succeed again.

The third rule states, "If it doesn't work, don't do it again. Do something different." The American work ethic promotes the concept that "If at first you don't succeed, try, try again." When trying again, it is important to use different strategies to yield different results. In counseling, however, when confronted with difficulties, clients tend to use the same familiar coping strategies because that is all they already know how to do. Walter and Peller (1992) describe a common example of this phenomenon, wherein people repeat ineffective strategies over and over. People often misplace an item such as a wallet or a set of keys. On searching for the item and not finding it on the kitchen table, they check the dresser in the bedroom unsuccessfully, followed by the counter in the bathroom, and then back to the kitchen table once again. If the item was not on the table before, why would it be there now? Repeating something that didn't work doesn't make sense; continued exploration in new locations is a more logical choice. Subscribing to this third rule helps counselors reformulate their ideas about resistance, because when clients demonstrate reluctance or appear uncooperative, they actually are telling counselors what does not work for them.

SOLUTION-FOCUSED ASSUMPTIONS

The basic philosophy of any counseling approach carries with it basic assumptions counselors need to internalize for the model to work. Adhering to these assumptions keeps the counselor on track. Various solution-focused practitioners articulate in their own way the assumptions inherent in the solution-focused approach. Walter and Peller (1992) are to be credited with the basics of the assumptions that follow.

The first assumption contends that when we concentrate on successes, beneficial changes will take place. The focus needs to be directed toward what is right and working for clients as opposed to what's wrong and troublesome. Practicing "solution talk" rather than "problem talk" facilitates the process. This is a rather difficult assignment for novice solution-focused counselors because most mental health providers have been conditioned to look for problems.

Shifting from problem to solution identification requires conscious effort and repeated practice.

Many years ago, this concept was exemplified in the forward-thinking work of Hosford, Moss, and Morrell (1976) with stuttering inmates. After recording conversations with prisoners, a second recording was made from the original with all stuttering edited out. The convicts listened to the edited recording that featured their talking without any trace of stuttering. Their stuttering was significantly reduced as a result of focusing on the positive and the solution rather than the problem. The same solution approach was implemented with a university basketball player to improve his free throw shooting. An edited video that demonstrated his shooting free throws with perfect form and accuracy was prepared. Prior to games and practice, he watched the tape, then closed his eyes and imagined himself shooting with perfect form. His habit of only focusing on the solution—an accurate shot—resulted in his missing only one free throw for the entire season!

The second assumption asserts that every problem has identifiable exceptions that can be found and transformed into solutions. Clients are inclined to view their problems as always happening, when, in reality, their problems fade away at times. Clients become so immersed with their issues that they often fail to see the instances when the problem isn't present. Clients fail to recognize the significance of these exceptions. It is up to counselors to listen carefully for hints that signal where, when, and how exceptions occur as a step in helping clients develop solutions.

Jean, a seventh-grade girl, requested help because she and her older sister, a junior in high school, didn't communicate often, and when they did, they constantly argued about who was right and who was wrong. Then, each tried to prove the other wrong with a report to their father. Jean desired to end this conflict.

After the counselor inquired about when their relationship was somewhat better, Jean recalled an incident 2 months earlier in which she and her sister talked about what was going on in their lives, and for a few days afterward, they didn't argue or report to their dad. Jean recalled that her sister even "took up for her" on one occasion. Although the exception was hard to find initially, with some probing it was rediscovered. Jean was assigned the task of doing more of what worked. In the second meeting a week later, Jean reported that she had been talking with her sister and had stopped telling on her, and her sister had responded similarly. They started to become allies and to do some things together. Jean's father remarked to Jean and her sister that he had noticed fewer quarrels and that he was happier seeing this. This was apparent to Jean as she noted that he began to smile more when he came home. The identifiable solutions were there all the time, hidden in the exceptions to Jean's problem. All it took to get Jean on track toward a healthier relationship with her sister was three meetings of teamwork between Jean and her counselor.

The third assumption is that small changes have a ripple effect that expands into larger changes. Once people get to know one another, they become somewhat predictable and come to anticipate each other's behaviors. When clients alter their behaviors ever so slightly, it causes a chain reaction in response to the initial change. Those affected by the change find themselves adjusting their responses, which in turn elicits further changes in clients. As in Jean's situation, when she became supportive of her sister, her sister became supportive of her. They began to do things with one another. The changes between the sisters also had an observable, positive effect on their father.

The fourth assumption recognizes that all clients have what it takes to resolve their difficulties. Who knows clients better—so why not use their expertise? By highlighting clients' strengths and how these strengths are initiated rather than focusing on deficits, changes occur more rapidly. Counselors and clients together face the task of fully exposing moments of success and, perhaps most important, identifying what clients have done to make these moments happen. Exploring clients' road maps to success steers them toward an empowering adventure.

After 3 weeks of using SFBC with at-risk middle school students, the school secretary reported that she had asked these students the same two questions. The first was, "Do you want to come back and see the counselor again?" They enthusiastically responded, "Yes, I would like to do that." And the follow-up question was, "Do you think he (the counselor) wants to see you?" They emphatically responded, "He sure does!" These students had gained confidence by recognizing they were capable of being successful and were ready to demonstrate they could do it again. Students seemed pleasantly surprised that a counselor or administrator would talk to them about what they were doing right, when their past experiences were generally negative because discussions focused on what they were doing wrong. A fourth-grade boy commented at the beginning of a second session, "I like coming here, for this is the first time anyone has talked to me about the things I do good." Friends of some of the students who had been counseled requested counseling for themselves and made comments such as, "Bridget isn't getting in trouble anymore, so I want you to fix me up like you did her." Accenting children's previously unrecognized resources challenges them to prove their competency.

The fifth assumption concludes that clients' goals are viewed in positive terms, reflecting what clients want to do, rather than in negative terms, reflecting the absence of something they don't want to do. It is unlikely that clients can picture something not happening. To do this, clients must envision something else occurring in its place. For example, try to imagine yourself not arguing with your parents. You will either see yourself arguing with them or see yourself doing something instead of arguing. Constructing a goal of *not* doing something is unproductive because it cannot be measured. As clients relate their goals in negative terms, recounting what they don't want, counselors are charged with helping clients identify positively worded goals that reflect what they do want to happen. Clients are empowered as they envision themselves accomplishing a measurable goal.

ADDITIONAL GUIDING CONCEPTS

In addition to the foregoing assumptions, several supplemental concepts provide a road map for implementing this model.

Concept 1: Avoid Problem Analysis

Philosopher Ludwig Wittgenstein once said, "It's a mistake to look for an explanation when all you need is a description of how things work" (source unknown). SFBC addresses what is working for children instead of exploring the etiology of their problems.

Rudy, a sixth-grade boy, was referred to me because he could not control his temper, which resulted in his cursing and fighting in school and in the trailer court where he lived. Because of his outbursts, his mother and stepfather were being threatened with eviction. Rather than embarking on an in-depth exploration of the causes of his temper, cursing, and fighting, we focused on when this wasn't a problem for him. This emphasis reinforced Rudy's ability to control himself.

Concept 2: Be Efficient With Your Interventions

One goal is to get clients in and out of counseling as quickly as possible. Typically, therapists spend much time trying to discover the source and cause of problems; in contrast, the solution-based counselors go for solutions that work. Counselors must avoid making clients dependent on them for long-term answers when all they may need is a nudge to start them on their path toward their own solutions. With time constraints often dictating school counselors' agendas, getting the most accomplished in a minimum number of interventions is essential.

A 13-year-old middle school boy named Derek saw a friend shoot himself in the head with a 22-caliber pistol. Four days after the incident, he requested counseling. With just a few interventions, Derek began to recognize solutions he already was doing occasionally. When he felt he needed to express his feelings about the incident, he was able to initiate a conversation with the victim and his mother. He also recognized that sometimes he needed to be physical, so he played basketball to relieve his tension. One meeting with Derek to identify the solutions that he already had started to construct was all it took to relieve his troubles.

Concept 3: Focus on the Present and Future

When counselors help clients identify what will have to happen in their world to tell them they no longer need counseling, it conveys the presupposition that things will be better in the future. Having clients paint this picture of how their present and future will look when they are successful and devoid of their problems sends a clear message that counselors believe in their clients' abilities to overcome their adversities. This also suggests to clients that counselors are concerned with their present and future adjustments. Past events are only emphasized in the process of finding exceptions to problems. In contrast, most conventional therapeutic approaches expect clients to investigate and understand the past as a precursor to changing their behavior. This can be so overwhelming to many clients that they use the past as a scapegoat to inhibit personal growth. Solution-focused counselors find that once clients begin to see themselves doing the desired behaviors, their perception of the past changes and exploring the past becomes unnecessary. Getting clients to take action first shows them that they are able to succeed regardless of previous obstacles.

James, an eighth-grade boy, was sent to me because of his low self-esteem. He had fallen off a bike when he was 8 years old and nearly died from the resulting head injury. He took longer than others his age to formulate responses to my questions. He spoke in a slow and deliberate manner, often saying that the questions I asked were hard to answer. However, given enough time, he was able to process information quite well. He was failing most of his classes, except for several D's. His goal for counseling was to stop feeling dumb and to feel smart sometimes. Focusing on the present, we searched for occasions when he felt a little less dumb or even a little smart. Additional interventions helped James identify what he was doing for himself to enable that to happen. He identified that he had been more successful and felt more okay about himself when he blocked out distractions in class so he could focus on what the teacher was saying. During one of our sessions I asked James how he was able to stay focused on our session when loud outside noises were permeating the room. After thinking about the question for a few moments he replied, to his amazement, "I watched your lips." He also reported feeling better about himself when he went to the library after school to do his homework instead of going home, and when he asked to be tutored during the last period of the day. James did improve several of his grades to D's and C's, and he even scored 100% on a science test for the first time. These improvements helped him feel smarter.

Concept 4: Focus on Actions Rather Than Insights

Children's levels of cognitive development limit their ability to comprehend insights about their problems. Insight development also requires a time commitment that students and counselors do not have. Furthermore, Metcalf (1995) points out that "knowing why we are the way we are doesn't offer solutions. As students discover why they are sad, angry or shy, they often use the information as a symptom and reason for not succeeding" (p. 19). As a result of Freud's influence, the psychological community has espoused the belief that clients need to know why they got to be the way they are and that this insight is required for change. Yalom (1995) argues against this position because he has found that insight is not necessary for change to occur.

I worked with a 12-year-old girl, Tiffany, who was referred because she repeatedly fought with other students and argued with and swore at her grandmother and her teachers. She was on the verge of being removed from the honors program and placed in a class for students with behavior disorders. Because her mother didn't want Tiffany, her grandmother was raising her. Many non-solution-focused counselors would have pursued insights surrounding her hostile behavior as it might relate to her mother's rejection. However, because Tiffany's goal was to get along better with classmates, teachers, and her grandmother, counseling targeted what she was doing (her actions) during the times when she was able to control her temper and get along even a little better with them. By our third meeting, she had improved so much that she was no longer being considered for the behavior disorder class and was asked to tutor some of the children with behavior disorders at a neighboring elementary school once a week. She was so effective that the elementary school behavior disorder teacher requested that Tiffany come to the school every day. Moreover, her grandmother was reported to have commented, "I like my new Tiffany better." Although Tiffany still had her ups and downs, her behavior and relationships improved significantly.

SUMMARY

SFBC has been shown to be an effective and efficient counseling approach (DeJong & Berg, 1998; LaFountain et al., 1996; Littrell,

Malia, & Vanderwood, 1995; Thompson & Littrell, 1998) that will enable school counselors and administrators to provide counseling to their students. By focusing on solutions rather than problems, counseling becomes brief. The emphasis on students' strengths and resources stimulates students' confidence.

PRACTICE EXERCISE

The following exercise will help you see the impact on clients when the interview shifts from a problem to a solution focus.

- Think of a recent problem that is causing you some difficulty. Answer the following questions about this problem:
  When did this problem begin?
  What seems to be the cause of this problem?
  How often does this problem occur?
  What keeps this problem going?
  What do you do to overcome this problem?

- Note the effect these problem-focused questions have on you.
  Are you left with a sense of direction about how to overcome your issue?
  Do your answers to these questions help you come to a resolution of this problem?
  As you think about what you have just experienced, are you left with feelings of hope or hopelessness?
  Do your answers leave you feeling empowered?

- Using the same problem, answer the following questions:
  When do you not experience this problem during problem times?
  What's different about the times when you don't have this problem?
  How do you explain that this problem doesn't happen then?
  How do you keep this from being a problem then?

- Note the effect these solution-focused questions have on you.
  Are you left with a sense of direction about how to overcome your issue?
  Do your answers to these questions help you come to a resolution of this problem?

As you think about what you have just experienced, are you left with feelings of hope or hopelessness?

Do your answers leave you feeling empowered?

- Notice the different reactions you experience when answering problem-oriented versus solution-oriented questions.

    Which ones seem to be more helpful to you?

    Which ones help you be more responsible?

    Which ones might lead to enhancing your self-esteem?

Your answers most likely would have led you to conclude that solution-focused questions were more productive for you and would be of more benefit to your students as well.

Setting Goals

To be efficient and effective with SFBC, well-developed goals need to be established with students. Identification of goals in the first interview, regardless of one's theoretical orientation, is the best predictor of effective counseling outcomes. Furthermore, the more concrete and behaviorally specific the goals, the more quickly clients improve. Goals also must be stated in terms of the small steps of observable actions students will start, not in terms of what they will not do or what they will stop. The solution-focused approach also calls for creating hypothetical goals that include the desired behaviors as a way to help students see what is possible for them.

OPENING THE FIRST MEETING: EXPLAINING THE PROCESS

As in any form of counseling, before beginning the first session with students, you first explain the procedures. This prepares students for the difficult questions you will ask, the note taking, and the break that will occur when you write a message for the student, which will be explained later. Clients learn the ways this form of brief counseling differs from other approaches they may have experienced or what they may have anticipated.

After a brief exchange of introductions and usual greetings, the procedures are introduced something like this:

I want to let you know how this is going to work. I am going to ask you a lot of questions, and some of them are going to sound kind of crazy and will be tough to answer [for some students, informing them that the questions will be hard to answer is intriguing and challenging]. Some of the answers you give I'm going to write down on my notepad and I'm going to use these notes to write you a message. At the end of our meeting, I will take a few minutes to review the notes and take some time to put my thoughts together about what we have discussed so I can write you a message. When I finish, I will tell you what I was thinking about and read the message to you. I will make a copy of the message so you can take one with you and I can keep one. What do you think about this?

This explanation introduces the process, acquaints students with procedures, and also prepares them for how hard they will have to work to answer difficult questions. When students get stuck, you can refer to this introduction by saying, "Remember what I said when we began about how hard it will be to answer some of these questions? Well, this is one of those questions." The last thing you want is for students to feel stupid because they are having difficulty answering questions. Interventions can be used to keep this from happening and, at the same time, build a supportive relationship.

Walter and Peller (1992) have suggested that counseling sessions begin with a question that initiates goal-oriented thinking soon after clients sit down. After exchanging greetings, they recommend asking, "What's your goal for coming here?" For some students, this works well because they can easily identify specific goals they would like to achieve in counseling. With other students, however, a brief social exchange is needed to break the ice before counseling can begin. And still others may wish to complain before getting down to business. When this occurs, it's best to let them "unload" for a brief time. You should acknowledge students' concerns by listening, reflecting empathetically, nodding, and making comments that demonstrate support for their coming to counseling.

To initiate the identification of goals in SFBC, typically you can ask, "What's the reason you have come to see me?" Or, "What will have to happen as a result of your coming here that will tell you that you no longer need to see me?" Or you may say, "How will you know when counseling is no longer necessary?" These questions elicit statements that can be developed into concrete behavioral goals.

DEVELOPING A GOAL: USING OUTCOME QUESTIONS THAT DETAIL SOLUTIONS IN POSITIVE TERMS

When students are asked about their goals for counseling, they respond in one of four ways. Students' goal statements can be classified as (a) positive goals, (b) negative goals, (c) harmful goals, or (d) "I don't know" goals.

Positive Goals

Positive goals state behaviors that can be observed and measured. Students who respond with positive goals may say, "I want to improve my grades, and I want you to help me to figure out how to do that." Or they may say, "I would like to learn how to get along better with the other kids." Or they may state, "I want to be able to get my teacher off my back so I don't have to come back to this stupid place again." These replies are general goals stated in terms of what students want to accomplish and therefore can be defined as positive goals. Positive goals are also measurable, so that students can recognize when their objectives have been attained.

However, most positive goals lack the concrete, specific behavioral details that can indicate when students are on track for reaching them. Eliciting descriptions of specific things students will be doing when they are moving in the right direction gives them the details needed to paint mental pictures of their solutions.

Consider the following questions to help students create their behaviorally specific goal pictures:

- "What do you think you would be doing that would tell you your grades were on the rise?" Or, "So as your grades are on the rise, what would you be doing that would have caused that to happen?"

- "What would the other kids in your class say you were doing that would show them that you're getting along better with them?" Or, "If you were getting along better with the other kids, what would you notice that you were doing to make it so?"
- "Tell me what you would be doing that would convince you that you're able to express your feelings to your parents?" Or, "When your parents observe you expressing your feelings to them, what would they say you would be doing that you're not doing yet?"

When students reply with nonspecific answers, you must continue to persist for details until the student describes a visual picture of the desired behavior. As indicated in the questions above, the tenor of your questions implies that students will accomplish their goals. The questioning follows a pattern—the answer to your follow-up question provides the information needed to form the next question, which in turn solicits additional examples of what students' goals look like to them and their significant others.

Negative Goals

Often, clients respond to counselors' inquiries with negative goals, which are goals expressed as the absence of something. Clients either want to avoid having something happen or they wish to stop something that has been happening. Negative goals are difficult, if not impossible, to attain. The critical perspective about negative goals involves realizing that for something to not happen, something else must take its place. Therein lies the goal.

Unfortunately, negative goals are more commonly expressed than positive goals. Typically, students express them in two ways: (a) wanting themselves to stop doing something or (b) wanting others to stop doing something. Each form of negative goal must be addressed separately.

When students want to stop doing something, ask them to identify the specific behaviors that will be substituted. Typical expressions of this kind of negative goal include, "I don't want to get bad grades," or "I don't want to lose my temper," or "I want to stop being late to class." It's best to reframe absence-of-something (negative) expressions into presence-of-something (positive) goals.

When students express this type of negative goal, immediately intervene with questions that solicit observable behavioral replacements. To redirect a negative goal into a positive one, it works to use questions like, "If you weren't doing _____, then what would you be doing instead/differently/in place of/rather than, or what would you start doing?"

Interventions to Help Reframe Negative Goals

More specifically, consider the following brief exchanges that redirect negative goals into positive ones (*C* = Counselor; *S* = Student):

Example 1

C: If you weren't getting bad grades, then what would you be doing instead?

S: I would be getting better grades. (Positive goal)

C: So if you were on the path to getting better grades, what would you be doing that would show that? (Specifics of goal)

Example 2

C: So instead of losing your temper, what would you be doing?

S: I would stay calm. (Positive goal)

C: Remaining calm is what you want. And what would you be doing that would tell you that you are calm? (Detailing the specifics of goal)

Example 3

C: So what would you be doing rather than being late to class?

S: I would go to class on time. (Positive goal)

C: Therefore, making sure you're in your classroom on time is your goal. What would you start doing that would indicate you were on the right track to getting to class on time? (Detailing the specifics of starting a goal)

As shown, the follow-up interventions enabled students to provide more details about what their goals looked like. The more behaviorally specific the goal, the better the chance clients can assess their successes.

More often than not, students express negative goals that call for others to be different or to stop doing certain things. This form of goal implies that others will need to change for clients to be happy and that counselors can help make that happen. It also implies that others must be the first to initiate change.

When students express goals that reflect a desire for others to stop something or not do something, help clients reframe their goals into positively stated goals that give the client the responsibility. Common examples of this pattern of negative goal statements are, "I don't want my parents to interfere with my choice of friends." Or "I don't want to be ignored when I have something to say in class." These rebuttals can be effective: "How can I help you with this?" "How is this a problem for you?" "What difference does that make to you?" "That seems really important to you. What's the reason for that?" "If they did change, what would that do for you?" Students begin to recognize their responsibilities when the goal is shifted to the positive.

Interventions When Students Want Others to Change

The following types of interventions are effective when students' proposed goals focus on changing the behavior of another person.

Example 1

C: So, if your parents didn't interfere with your choice of friends, what would that do for you?

S: Then I would be more comfortable talking to my parents about the things that I'm doing.

C: So, becoming comfortable talking to your parents about what's going on with you is what you would like to happen? (Positive goal)

S: Yeah, I'd like that because we used to talk all the time.

C: So, when you become a little more comfortable talking to them, what would you be doing that's different from what you're doing now? (Detailing specifics of goal)

Example 2

C: What can I do to help you with this problem (being ignored in class)?

S: Maybe you can tell my teacher how I'm feeling ignored when I want to contribute.

C: So, you would like her to know that you want to be more involved in class and you're looking for ways to make her aware of this. (Positive goal)

S: Yes. I would tell her, but I'm uncomfortable.

C: You're saying that if you were more comfortable, you would let her know on your own, and I'm wondering what you would be doing that would show you that you are just a little more comfortable. (Detailing specifics of goal)

Determining the client's motivation for wanting others to stop doing or not do something enables you to help the student identify the underlying positive goal for counseling.

Harmful Goals

When first beginning to use SFBC with students, you may encounter situations that throw you off track. Often, when this occurs, you will switch to what you know best and the counseling or other approaches you typically use. Being prepared for impediments that may surface in an interview helps you to avoid abandoning the solution-focused model.

The solution-focused approach emphasizes that the goals for counseling must be the student's, not the counselor's. On rare occasions, students present goals that, if fulfilled, would violate the law, be harmful to them, or not be in their best interests. Examples include underage students dropping out of school, wanting to have babies, becoming prostitutes, hurting someone, damaging property, running away from home, and so forth. Obviously, ethical counselors and administrators do not support harmful goals.

Always recognize that students' destructive goals are really symptoms of underlying or root goals that reflect students' needs to fill voids in their lives. Using a series of solution-finding questions that identify the reasons for their goals helps students reframe and identify healthy goals that will meet their underlying needs. Addressing harmful goals is similar to working with impossible goals.

The following example illustrates how to modify destructive goals into productive goals.

C: What's your goal?

S: I don't want to go to school anymore.

C: What's the reason you don't want to go to school anymore?

S: Because I'm flunking all my classes, and I've just given up trying.

C: So, are you also saying that if you were trying harder and were doing better in school, you would be more satisfied?

S: Probably so.

C: Could a goal for you be to figure out a way to try harder and do better in school?

S: Yes, I would like that.

C: What would be your first clue that you were trying harder?

S: I would go to class.

This example demonstrates how, by paying careful attention to the clues students divulge, this information can be used to redirect an unproductive goal into a productive one.

"I Don't Know" Goals

Students often are referred to counselors and administrators by parents, teachers, and other invested adults. The real customers for change are those who referred the student. Unfortunately, the customers don't seek counseling for themselves but want counselors to change the student, who most often is a noncommitted visitor. When visitors are asked about their goals for counseling, "I don't know" responses are common. On hearing this response, many counselors become stuck. The use of hypothetical *if* questions frequently helps visitors begin to develop goals. The examples in Table 2.1 demonstrate this technique.

Table 2.1   Questions to Help Students Set Goals

Goal Question	Student Response	Counselor Response
What's your goal?	I don't know.	If you did know, . . .
What's the reason you're here?	I have no idea.	If you did have an idea, . . .
Who do you think sent you?	I can't figure it out.	If you could figure it out, . . .
What's the reason someone wants you to be here?	Beats me.	If you could guess, . . .
What would your mom say you would be doing that would tell her you don't need to see me anymore?	It's beyond me.	If it weren't beyond you, . . .

Inserting a hypothetical *if* removes the pressure of having to know the correct answer. When the hypothetical approach is used, most students are willing to identify the reason for being sent to you. In some cases, persistent repetition of *if* questions may be needed to ascertain the reasons the client is in your office.

Concrete behavioral goals are often not fully defined in the initial phase of goal identification. To expedite this, you can help students explore hypothetical solutions using a type of all-purpose strategy called the "miracle question."

THE MIRACLE QUESTION

The seeds of solutions have been planted during the initial contact with clients as school counselors engage in solution and goal talk rather than problem talk. Focusing on what life would look like if students were reaching their goals or were free of their problem helps highlight unnoticed successes. The miracle question magnifies and exposes minute glimpses of solutions not apparent when viewing the total puzzle. Fitting each piece of the puzzle together constructs a large picture in which exceptions can be found. The miracle question was discovered by deShazer (1990) in his frustration with a client's inability to formulate a well-defined, realistic, and achievable goal. It has since become a valuable tool for solution-focused counselors.

Typically, the miracle question is stated as follows:

Suppose when you go to sleep tonight, a miracle occurs, and because you are sleeping, you don't know it happens. The miracle solves the problem that brought you here. When you wake up in the morning, what clues will you see that lead you to discover that this miracle has taken place? What will you notice you will be doing differently?

deShazer found that not only was his initial client able to come up with a well-defined goal in response to this question but it worked with other clients as well. The miracle question was so effective in establishing well-defined goals that it has become part of the solution-focused brief therapy model.

This question has been found to work with most students, although its use is limited with younger children who cannot conceptualize the notion of miracles. Altering the question may help some younger children understand what is being asked. An alternative might be, "If I had a magic wand (magic lamp) and was to wave (rub) it over your head and the problem that brought you here disappeared, what would be different and what would you see yourself doing?" For students who have difficulty answering miracle and magic wand questions, the following hypothetical question may be effective: "Picture yourself 6 months from now and the problem that brought you here has been solved. What would be different about you that would tell you that we no longer need to meet?" After asking this initial, hypothetical miracle question, persistently use the client's own words to fine-tune the responses until the goals are well developed.

Nonspecific Miracles

Often students give answers that aren't behaviorally specific, and their answers must be clarified:

S: If this miracle happened, I'd wake up in the morning and I'd be happier.

C: And when you are happier, what would you be doing (specific actions) that would tell you that you are happier?

S: Well, I guess I'd be smiling more. I guess I'd be talking more to my brother in a friendly way.

C: And when you're talking in a friendlier way, what would your brother see you doing that would tell him that?

S: I would say hello to him in the morning and maybe even ask him if he was doing anything special that day.

C: So, if that happened, how would your brother respond to you?

S: He would probably tell me, and we would talk about the things we would both be doing that day.

C: So, those are some of the clues that would tell you that you are happier. Who else would notice that you are happier?

As the sequence progressed, vague expressions of goals were detailed with specific behavioral descriptions. Questions also elicited the reactions of others who would notice changes taking place (reciprocal relationship questions). Helping students envision the ripple effects of their efforts reinforces their desire to initiate positive actions. The miracle question helps redirect students from problems to solutions. By detailing the concrete behaviors students will be doing to make their goals become a reality, hope rather than hopelessness is engendered as forgotten possibilities are rediscovered.

Changing behaviors changes students' views of the events, which, in turn, changes their feelings. The solution-focused approach differs from some other counseling approaches in that it builds on the belief that changes in behavior lead to changes in feelings. This contrasts with a more traditional counseling approach that assumes affective changes precede behavioral changes.

Another vague response to the miracle question that is typical of students is, "I'd be doing my work." You then follow up with one or more of these questions: "Doing your work, what do you mean 'doing your work'? Can you tell me what that would look like?" "If I had a video camera and I were videotaping you, what would I be seeing you doing?" "What would your parents see you doing that would tell them you were doing your work?" "What would your teachers be reporting to me that would convince them that you are doing your work?" "If I were to walk outside your classroom door, what would I see you doing that would tell me that you were doing your work?" "If your classmates were seeing you doing your work, what would they say they were seeing you do?" At this stage, specific concrete behavioral responses are sought and developed, resulting in video-like process responses. For example, the student might respond, "I'd be sitting in my desk, I'd be looking at the teacher, and I'd be writing down notes." Students' answers provide them with a so-called mental video of themselves accomplishing successful concrete goals.

Some students need help describing concrete behaviors when trying to detail their goals. For example, a student whose goal is to learn to pay attention in class may be stuck in describing actions to accomplish this goal. To help the student give a more detailed description, you could ask, "So when you are paying attention, what would your eyes be doing? When you are paying attention, what would your feet (hands, eyes, etc.) be doing?"

Impossible or Improbable Miracles

Students may respond to a hypothetical solution question with an impossible or improbable goal. They may want their divorced parents to reunite, deceased relatives to come back to life, or friends who have moved away to move back. They realize counselors can't do anything to bring about these changes, but if this miracle happened, that would be their answer. A student's sense of loss often underlies these wishes. Discovering the underlying needs helps clients identify realistic goals in place of impossible or improbable wishes. Helpful questions can yield more realistic goals. For example, you might ask, "That seems to mean a lot to you because . . . ?" "What about this is so important to you?" In the example of the student wanting his parents reunited, the dialogue might go as follows:

C: What difference would it make to you if that happened?

S: Then our whole family would be together again.

C: And what would having your whole family together do for you?

S: I would feel part of the family.

C: So, feeling like you're part of the family is a goal for you!

S: Yes, I want that. (This now becomes the goal.)

The counselor then uses the following kinds of questions to identify the behaviors that will indicate to the student that this goal is being achieved: "When you were feeling like you're part of the family, what would you find yourself doing that would tell you this was happening?" or "If your father were noticing you feeling that you were part of the family, what would he say he would see you doing?"

Another example illustrates working with unlikely miracles:

C: So, you really miss your grandmother since she died. What's the thing you miss the most?

S: She made me feel comfortable to talk to her when I had something on my mind, and she would really listen to me.

C: So, being comfortable with someone to talk to who really listens when you have something on your mind is what you would like to have happen?

S: Yes.

C: What would tell you that you were comfortable talking to someone about the things on your mind?

S: I would be relaxed.

C: And if you were relaxed, what would you be doing that would tell you this?

S: I would be sitting on the floor, looking in the other person's eyes.

C: If you were doing this, what would the person do in return?

S: They would be looking right in my eyes and talking in a soft voice.

"I Want Others to Be Different" Miracles

Students may also describe their miracles as wanting others to change because they view them as the problem. Students commonly think others must be the first to alter their behaviors before students will adjust their own behaviors. You will need to help students understand reciprocity—the notion that changes in one's own behavior produce behavior changes in others. You can use these concepts to the client's advantage by applying the miracle question process in a way that helps students recognize that they can initiate behavior changes. The following example illustrates how the miracle question can be used in this situation:

S: You say "miracles." Well, if that were to happen, my teacher would start treating me fairly like he does the other kids.

C: So, suppose this miracle did occur, and the teacher was now treating you fairly like the other kids, what would that look like?

S: He would call on me when I raise my hand.

C: So, if he called on you when you raised your hand, what would you start doing differently?

S: I wouldn't talk in class without permission.

C: So, what would you be doing instead?

S: I would sit in my seat and look at the teacher, or be writing down what he says with my lips sealed.

C: What do you think he will do when he sees you acting this way?

S: He will probably treat me like the other kids.

C: Is that what you want to have happen?

S: I sure do.

C: So, doing those things you just described could possibly result in your teacher changing as well.

Helping students see the reciprocal cause and effect of small changes in their own behavior enables them to see possibility for change in others.

Detailed answers are important. Students' answers need to generate the specifics of how solutions can happen. Using the hypothetical perceptions of others is an effective method for developing details. You can use interventions such as these: "If I were observing you . . . , what would I see?" "If your parents, teachers, and friends were noticing you . . . , how would they describe it to me?" These are the important details that create pictures for students. Students can begin to see the ripple effect of their own behaviors when you and the student engage in interchanges such as this:

C: When you are being friendlier by smiling and saying "hello" first, what would your sister do in return?

S: She would smile and maybe start a conversation.

C: And when that happens, what would you do then?

The realization that changing one's behavior will result in others changing theirs is significant. This contrasts sharply with students' common belief that others have to change first. As noted earlier, of special importance is the knowledge that small changes lead to large changes and to more changes. Understanding these relationships helps clients move beyond the details of the small view to see the big picture. Students are empowered when they discover that they can initiate change in others by first initiating change in themselves.

"WHAT ELSE" QUESTIONS

Another technique can be used to enhance the chance that students will find instances of success and exceptions to problems. This is accomplished by asking, "What else will happen after this miracle has occurred?" You then use the same procedures as with the miracle question to elicit behavioral details. Repeating this sequence three or four times opens additional doors for students to expand their portraits of life without the problems.

ESTABLISHING WELL-DEVELOPED GOALS

Throughout the miracle-questioning sequence, goals should be stated as the presence of something or start of something (positive goal) rather than the absence of something or end of something (negative goal). Well-developed goals are described in concrete, behavioral terms that state in detail what the student will be doing when accomplishing the goal. Using *what* questions elicits answers that describe positive goal behaviors. As an example, a student has indicated that his goal is to be doing his work in class. But this goal is not specific enough to qualify as a well-developed goal. His description of work is vague, lacking details that would tell him that he has behaviorally achieved his goal. To clarify, you may ask, "What would you be doing that would show both you and your teacher that you were doing your work?" Or, "If I were sitting in your class watching you doing your work, what would I see you doing?" His response might be, "My book would be open, and I would be looking at the teacher." These two behaviors—keeping his book open and looking at the teacher—serve as observable, measurable objectives that will lead to accomplishing his goal.

Another student may indicate that her goal is to be happy when she is at school. Happy is not specific enough. You need to find what it will take to make the student happy by asking, "What will you be doing that will tell you that you are happy in school?" Or, "If your teacher were seeing you being happy in her class, what would she say she saw you doing?" Answers to these questions provide observable goals stated as the presence of something that can be replicated and recognized when achieved.

Well-developed goals also describe *how* students will move toward their goals. Describing goals in process form gives a video-like quality that helps clients visualize themselves taking the steps toward their goals. Asking *how* questions encourages students to describe goals with verbs ending in *ing* or with sequences of action. This, in turn, produces a video-like image that captures possibilities clients may have not envisioned previously. Following through with the earlier example, the student who described his goal as doing his work by having his book open and looking at the teacher could be asked, "How would you do that?" His answer might be, "I would be bringing my book to class and putting it on my desk and opening it up to the right page, and I would be watching the teacher." The student who wants to be happy, as demonstrated by her having her head up and answering questions that may be asked of her, could be queried, "How will the teacher know this is happening?" Her reply might be, "She would see me looking at her and the other students, and she would notice that I am raising my hand when she asks questions." See Table 2.2 for guidelines and phrases to help in establishing well-developed goals.

Well-developed goals tend to be small. In other words, they need to be manageable and reachable so students avoid feeling frustrated, discouraged, or overwhelmed. By keeping goals small, students will be able to recognize small changes. In contrast, with large goals that call for significant changes, students may fail to notice the small but significant indications of progress. Their attention to the big picture minimizes and may even conceal the small steps of progress along the way. The student examples presented thus far clearly illustrate small goals calling for small changes that students can easily recognize.

Table 2.2   Establishing Well-Developed Goals

Guideline	*Language*
State in positive rather than negative terms as the presence of a behavior or the start of something.	If you were not getting upset, what would you be doing instead or differently? What's the first thing you would be doing that would tell you you're on target?
Describe in concrete, detailed behavioral terms.	When you're being friendly, what would you be doing that would show that?
Express in process terms.	How have you managed to make that happen in spite of all the pressure? How will you be doing that?
Frame as being the client's responsibility, using his or her jargon.	What would you be doing differently that would show you were mellow?

Case Study: Using the Miracle Question

The following is one of several case studies, taken from actual cases, that will be presented throughout the book to demonstrate components of the solution-focused model. In this example Sue, a 13-year-old eighth-grade middle school student, is working to set goals. Her reason for seeing me was to improve her relationship with her mother by being more honest with her. Sue also wanted to be able to avoid doing things with her friends that got her in trouble (C = Counselor; S = Sue).

C: Here is the first strange question I'm going to ask you: Suppose a miracle happened during the night when you went to bed, and when you woke up in the morning, all your problems with your mom and you were solved. You didn't know the miracle happened because you were sleeping. What would be the first thing in the morning that you would notice—the first small sign that would say this miracle has happened?

S: Probably, my mom would say, "Do you want to go out tonight with your friends and do something with them?" because she told me it would take her awhile to trust me because I lied to her this weekend. She'd probably say, "I trust you now."

Sue's answer to the miracle question emphasized gaining her mother's trust; therefore, it was necessary to get Sue to provide the details describing what she would be doing that would cause her mother to trust her.

C: What would she say you would be doing for her to be saying that?

S: I'd have to build her trust back up in me. I'd have to take it one day at a time, and I would have to prove to her that I don't run no more and just prove to her that I can be trusted and not be doing stuff behind her back.

Her response still does not indicate the details of her behaviors that would show her mother what she will be doing; therefore, it is important to solicit the specific actions Sue will be taking.

C: How would she know that? What would she say would be the first thing she would notice about you that would tell her you could now be trusted?

S: I would be truthful with her. If she asks me a question, I tell her the truth.

Once a specific behavioral response is provided by the client, additional answers to the miracle question are sought.

C: What else would your mother notice after this miracle?

S: She would notice I've changed because of how I act.

C: How would she know that? What would she tell me had changed?

S: That my attitude has gone away and that me and her were spending more time together than we used to. And I wouldn't ask her to let me do things that I know she wouldn't want me to do. 'Cause I always pressure her, like "Please, Mom, please." So, if she says "no," I'll accept her answer.

C: All those things would certainly tell her that she could trust you more. What else would you see happening that would tell her this miracle had taken place?

S: I would spend more time with my mom. I wouldn't roll my eyes and not argue and accept her answers when she says "no" to me.

C: So, instead of rolling your eyes and giving your little voice, you'd be doing what?

S: I would say, "It's okay, that's fine," and I'd just go on and do what I was doing.

C: Okay. That would be one thing. Another thing that would tell you is that you would spend more time . . . with her.

S: We would sit down and watch TV together 'cause I used to always be in my room talking on the phone. We would just share more moments together.

C: You also said rather than argue, you would accept her answer when she says "no" to you. What do you mean by that?

S: I would just go, "Okay, that's fine. I won't go. I'll go somewhere else. If it will feel better to you then, if you don't want me to go there then. If you don't want me to go there so you won't worry about me then" and just accept it. I'll go somewhere else where I can go.

C: What is the first small sign that will tell you this miracle has happened?

S: I wouldn't go around the house yelling at my mom. I would just go, "Hi, Mom. How was your day at work? What are you all doing? Do you want to go do something?" And when Mom asks me to go outside and feed the cat, I'd say, "Sure, I'll feed the cat, the birds, and put the dog out." I used to be like, "Yeah, sure. I don't feel like feeding no cat." I could even fold towels 'cause I hate folding towels. Like she used to always ask me to fold the towels real quick, and I'd be like talking on the phone or watching TV. "No, I'm not folding no towels for you."

C: What would happen if you did all these things?

S: My mom would be like, "Are you sick?" and she would start trusting me and let me go out with my friends again.

SUMMARY

SFBC emphasizes establishing well-developed goals that are detailed in concrete behavioral terms. Goal development is further enhanced by asking hypothetical solution questions. The key hypothetical question associated with this approach is the miracle question. The miracle question provides a means for students to fantasize about what life would be like without their problems or what life would be like if they were attaining their goals.

Chapter 3 presents the next steps in the SFBC process. These steps include discovering exceptions or instances of success that have gone unrecognized, assessing how these exceptions or successes were made to occur, using scales to evaluate progress, and constructing a message that includes a homework task.

PRACTICE EXERCISE

Think about some problem that has been bothering you— something you want to stop happening. Answer the following questions about your situation.

- What would you like to see yourself do instead of what you are presently doing?
- Suppose tonight when you go to sleep, a miracle happens while you are sleeping so you are unaware the miracle has occurred. However, when you wake up, the problem you identified earlier is no longer a problem. What would you notice you would be doing differently that would tell you this miracle had occurred?
- If you noticed that you were no longer doing something you wanted to stop doing, what would you be doing in place of what you wanted to stop doing?

- Who would be the first to notice any of these things you are now doing instead?
- How would they respond to you when they notice your different behavior?
- How would you respond to them in return?

By answering these questions, you would have partially experienced the goal-setting segment of the SFBC process—the segment that precedes the steps described in Chapter 3: identifying exceptions, scaling, and constructing a message.

CHAPTER THREE

Discovering and Constructing Solutions

O nce hypothetical pictures of success are developed and magnified, the next step is to look for instances when small pieces of students' miracles have already happened. These expressions of exceptions fall in two categories: (a) instances when some segments of students' goals are being attained and (b) situations when the students' problems are less severe or are absent altogether. Both categories arise when identifying solutions.

When discovering and constructing solutions, students' attention should be directed to instances when improvements, however small, are happening. Even moments when students report they are a little less sad or upset or slightly less unsuccessful indicate a solution is present. Because students typically overlook their small successes, or "problemless" moments, these positive occurrences fade from memory. "Problems ignored grow, solutions ignored disappear." This so aptly describes what most clients experience. Therefore, rediscovering unrecognized, recurring solutions is the task for counselors and students.

Solution-focused counselors firmly believe that all students experience times when they are being successful or they are not encountering their problems. As an example, consider students who are seeking to live a healthy lifestyle instead of taking drugs. Even one time when they experienced the urge to use drugs but told themselves, "I'll skip it and wait another hour"—this is a repeatable solution. Answering the query, "How did you make it happen for this one time?" empowers students as they recognize their resources. Counselors can then offer support and reinforcement in the form of cheerleading in recognition of students' efforts.

REDISCOVERING UNRECOGNIZED SOLUTIONS

It is important to introduce this step to students by conveying the notion that some parts of the student's miracle already have taken place. This demonstrates your belief in the student's resources. Listen carefully to students' comments to catch words and phrases that imply things are working for them. Even more important, you must train students to listen for their own successes rather than failures. Students who are failing every class except one are exhibiting signs of some success in the class they are passing. In keeping with a solution-based approach, you need to focus on the class the student is passing and how the student is making that happen. Listening for even slight grades of difference furnishes clues to the student's resources for success.

Students' language can hold the key to spotting these small successes. Phrases or words such as *most of the time, nearly always, sometimes,* or *generally* suggest exceptions. For example, if the problem is there most of the time, then it implies that the problem is not present at least some of the time. Focusing on times when problems are a little less severe or when failure is not as pronounced also indicates successes that can be developed. You can help students recognize the presence of solutions by reframing their views of their situation.

Just as in general counseling, closed questions—those that can be easily answered "no"—are to be avoided. Questions that begin with *are, could,* or *can* may limit clients' ability to spot exceptions (e.g., "Are there times when some of this miracle is already happening?" or "Can you recall a time when this miracle took place even a little?" or "Could you tell me when this miracle has already happened?"). This sort of phrasing implies that there may or may not be times when the miracle is happening. Because solutions tend to evaporate when overlooked, clients habitually have trouble identifying exceptions to their difficulties.

The answer lies in phrasing the "exception question" with the presupposition that some of the miracle already has transpired. This helps students stretch their minds to find instances of success. The interview process to this point sends a strong message to students that you trust them to identify their own goals for counseling and believe they are capable of envisioning what their lives would be like without the problem. From those seeds, you now expect clients to develop the capacity to see their successes. Interventions that begin with "Tell me about sometimes when," "I would like to know when," "How close have you come to," or "The last time some part of" imply some degree of success has occurred.

The following case illustrates the discovery of instances of success. Maria is a 10-year-old elementary school student in the fifth grade who was constantly worried about her mother's hospitalizations. Her mother was diagnosed as having a bipolar mood disorder, and her mood swings scared Maria. Maria's schoolwork suffered because of her habitual thoughts about her mother. Her goal for counseling was to replace her negative thoughts with more pleasant ones. In exploring instances when she had enjoyable thoughts, Maria talked about riding her bike, playing games with her mother and friends, reading and writing at school, and the time she was able to "click off" her negative thoughts so she could have more pleasant ones. The focus immediately went to the time she was able to click off negative thoughts and subsequently click on positive thoughts. Highlighting this significant event helped Maria remember how she made this happen for herself. She recalled changing her thoughts from worrying about her mother to sports, music, and school. This was a resource that could now be replicated as needed.

After noting instances of achievement, the process continues by detailing the behavioral specifics of the exception. Helping students recall the features of their resources promotes a sense of accomplishment.

Patience and prodding may be necessary to identify exceptions for some students who may say, "I don't know" or claim, "I don't think it's ever happened." You may reply, "Now think about that for a minute before you answer so quickly. When has that happened even just a little bit?" Sometimes "microscoping," by focusing on what happened that week, day, or hour helps students identify triumphs. Verbally sharing your notes about how students described their miracles provides a quick review from which to draw exceptions.

Mac is a sixth-grade boy who had been in trouble repeatedly at school for breaking rules and failing his classes. His goal was to start following school rules and improve his grades. When asked about when some of his miracle had taken place, he responded, "That miracle hasn't happened" (*C* = Counselor; *M* = Mac).

C: Now think about it, Mac, for just a minute. How about today; when has it happened today just a little bit?

M: *(Pause.)* Well, you know, I guess it has. When I left the library today, the teacher asked us to walk in a straight line. I did.

C: Is that different?

M: Oh yeah, I'm usually bouncing off the lockers all the time. Oh yeah, in the lunchroom today, I ran and you're not supposed to run in the lunchroom. The teacher called me back, and I came back and I walked.

C: Is that different for you?

M: Oh yeah, I usually keep going. I don't ever come back. Then they get mad and chase me down and put me in detention.

Through persistence, Mac was able to identify times when moments of his miracle were happening. He couldn't think of any instances of this at first; however, focusing on events of that day enabled him to identify exceptions.

EMPOWERING THROUGH RECOGNITION OF STUDENTS' RESOURCES

Once instances of success are identified, students can then discover how they took these steps toward their miracles. As students understand how they bring about changes, a "mindmap" develops, showing them paths to their goals.

Mindmapping

Mindmapping refers to the creation of a road map of thoughts that guides individuals to their destination. Mindmaps are built by recalling and reinforcing instances when clients' behaviors led to success, however small. This creates a sort of imprint of thoughts about what succeeds. Mindmapping seeks to reinforce thought patterns that will ultimately create what might be called productive habits—habitual ways of behaving successfully in areas that caused difficulty in the past. Recognizing their resources, responsibilities, and strengths is the first step in helping students feel empowered to take charge of themselves.

Some interventions that develop mindmaps to solutions are as follows:

- "How did you manage to do that?"
- "What was different about this (or that) time?"
- "What did you do to make it work for you then?"
- "How do you account for these changes?"
- "That's so different. What brought that about in you?"
- "What kind of different thoughts were you having then?"
- "How did you do it?"

Mindmap questions are sometimes difficult to answer. "I don't know" replies can be addressed with "If you did know" responses. As noted in Chapter 2, asking *if* questions this way lessens the pressure to come up with the right answer, thus providing students the freedom to explore possibilities. Patient persistence in rephrasing this question often elicits answers students can use to educate themselves about how to meet their goals.

Sometimes students give the credit to someone else for their accomplishments. Shift responsibility for success to the student by using the "I bet you have been told that before and it didn't make any difference" intervention. The following example describes this intervention (*C* = Counselor; *S* = Student).

C: Tell me about a time when you were tempted not to do your schoolwork, but you did it anyway. How did you do it? How did you manage to make that happen?

S: My teacher told me that I had better do my work or I won't amount to anything. (With this explanation, the responsibility of doing his work this time was the teacher's.)

C: You know, I bet you've heard that before from your teacher, haven't you?

S: Yeah!

C: And you still didn't do your work?

S: Yeah!

C: So today was different. What made today different for you?

S: I decided that I'm as smart as the other kids, so I can do it.

C: So, that was a new decision for you. How did you make that decision this time?

S: I told myself I want to pass to the fifth grade, so I did my assignment.

This intervention caused the student to realize he was the one responsible for his success. Another path could have been followed in this situation—to determine how the student was able to listen seriously to the teacher this time and heed her advice. You might have said, "So you often hear that from your teacher, and it goes in one ear and out the other. But today was different; you really listened to her. How were you able to do that this time?"

Cheerleading

Supporting and encouraging students' success with praise is called *cheerleading.* Students love to be acknowledged for their accomplishments, especially those students in need of counseling. Their worlds are abundant with comments that stress what's wrong with them. Discovering what is right with them and letting them know about it uplifts their outlook and boosts their self-esteem. Any instance of success or exceptions to problems, regardless of how small, warrants recognition. You can communicate cheerleading by these means:

- Increasing the level of your voice to show how moved you are by students' efforts
- Expressing excitement when a new behavior is attempted

- Demonstrating that you are impressed with the maturity of students' thoughts or actions
- Expressing amazement with students' creative thinking or decision making
- Showing admiration for students' dedication and commitment to sticking with their new behaviors and not giving up

Be careful not to patronize students when cheerleading. It's essential that you truly mean what you express to your students; otherwise, your comments will appear insincere, negating everything that has been accomplished in the interview. The cheerleading will come across as more sincere when the specific reason for the praise is included in the cheerleading response. Using the word *because* is recommended when you cite the reason for the compliment as one of several ways to make the compliment more sincere and believable to the student. The following are some examples of cheerleading leads:

> "Wow! How did you manage to do . . . , *because* that showed courage."

> "That's amazing that you could . . . , *because* that shows how mature you are."

> "I'm really impressed with how you . . . , *because* that indicates that you can make great decisions."

> "How did you figure that out? Most kids your age couldn't do that."

> "Did you say you were only 11 years old? But you think like a 14-year-old."

> "How can you be that smart when you're only 7 years old?"

> "How were you able to come up with those thoughts? Most kids your age wouldn't be able to think that clearly."

> "That's unbelievable that you could remain calm under those circumstances, *because* most people would have lost it, but you didn't."

Comments such as these reinforce successful attempts and encourage repeated efforts.

The following excerpt of the interview with Sue, which was begun in the previous chapter, illustrates mindmapping, instances of success, cheerleading, and reciprocal relationship interventions (*C* = Counselor; *S* = Sue).

C: Hmm. You've got some good ideas. You really do. Tell me about some times when some of this miracle is already happening.

S: Last night.

C: Really! Tell me about that.

S: I was playing Nintendo, and Mom asked me, "Can I interrupt you for a minute?" And I go, "Yeah, sure." And she goes, "Can you feed the cat real quick for me?" and I was like, "Yeah, sure." 'Cause she was like folding towels and cooking supper and then I came in and she was folding towels and the pot was over boiling and I was like, "It's okay. I'll get it for you." And she was like, "Are you sure?" and I was like, "Yeah."

C: Well, what made that possible, because usually you wouldn't do that?

S: Uh huh. I don't know. Probably, because I want me and my mom to get along and stuff.

C: How thoughtful that was on your part, because you realized this would help you to get along if you cooperated with her and helped her.

S: Uh huh. And then one day, she asked me if I had any dirty clothes in my room. I said, "Yeah," and she was like, "Can you get them out for me?" What am I going to do, say, "No, not now. Why don't you come and get them?" Nah, so I said, "Yeah, sure. I'll get them out." Usually I'd be like, "No, I don't want to."

C: Gosh, I'm impressed, you just did it, and you didn't give her a hassle, because that shows how committed you are to getting along better with your mom.

S: Right. I didn't even say, "Hold on a second," and she didn't have to remind me or anything.

C: Wow! How did she react when you did that?

S: "Oh, thanks, honey! You are really helping me out a lot." And she was like, "Are you feeling okay?"

C: *(Laughing.)* That's the fever reaction.

S: Like when she asked me to go feed the cat and stop playing my Nintendo game. She was like, "Are you feeling okay? You stopped the game for me."

C: And when she did that, how did you respond to her?

S: "Yeah, Mom. I'm feeling okay. I'm just trying to help you out."

C: You told her you just wanted to help her out?

S: Uh huh.

Incidents when students achieve their goals and instances when they are problem free suggest solutions are present. Illuminating these times helps student recognize their resources. Through mindmapping, methods students use to bring about their solutions are explored and reinforced through praising and cheerleading their efforts.

SCALING A BASELINE AND PROGRESS

Scaling is the next step in the sequence and is used to determine where students are in terms of the goals they have set. Students are asked to rate themselves on a scale from 0 (lowest) to 10 (highest) with respect to attainment of their goals. This provides a baseline to measure progress. Students' assessments typically reflect some level of success because they generally report scores greater than 0. Ratings above 0 suggest that things have been worse in the past, and something has been done to make them better. Helping students identify how they made things better empowers them to recognize their resources. In those rare cases when students report they are at 0, you can remind students that coming in for counseling indicates willingness to work and desire to make things better. Discovering how they have come to believe that things could be better reflects hope and progress.

Asking students what they will be doing when they move up one number on the scale helps them to identify the actions needed to make progress toward their goals. When students answer the miracle question and questions about instances of success, they see possibilities they may not have been able to construct otherwise.

Scaling Techniques for Measuring Baseline Goal Attainment

One issue within the counseling field is the difficulty with measuring outcomes. The scaling method used with SFBC provides a means to quantify clients' progress. With scaling, students rate themselves on a scale from 0–10, with 10 being the day after their miracles have happened and the problems that brought them to counseling have been solved and 0 being when things were at their absolute worst. In terms of this continuum, where are they right now? Typically, clients tend to classify themselves between a 2 and a 4. Often the counseling interview itself causes improvement because the student begins to realize successes that were previously unrecognized. Ratings above 0 indicate that things have been worse; therefore, something is better now, even if only a little. Identifying what is better or working and how students are causing that to happen points out the solutions already available to them.

Soliciting information from students about how they have reached their ratings on the scale helps them understand where they are and how they arrived there. The same sort of questioning process is used. Cheerleading also reinforces successes.

Children 5–7 years old may have difficulty discriminating among numbers. Using a smaller scale with fewer choices or a series of 10 faces (with numbers under them), with a pronounced frown on one end and a pronounced smile on the other end, may work more effectively. A 12-inch ruler also may be used. Younger children tend to be more visual and have an easier time identifying their rating on scales using props such as these.

Clients rarely respond to the scaling question with a 0 rating. If it should happen, focus on the student's presence in your office as reflecting anticipation of making things better. How did the student decide to come to see you in spite of the seemingly hopeless situation? How did the student manage to get out of bed, get cleaned up and dressed, catch the school bus, get to class, and show up at your door that morning? These actions say something about a desire to improve things. What gives the student the idea that there is even hope to resolve the difficulties? Ask why the student is not at a minus 10—how is the student able to do as well as he or she is doing? In other words, asking why things are not worse than they are suggests students have the ability to cope. The coping strategies students use to just get through their days are actually solutions that need to be developed.

Identifying the Behaviors Leading to Improvement

Once students have assessed their placement on the scale of 0–10 and discussed how they made it happen and the reciprocal effect of their actions, ask them to explore small steps toward improvement. This is done by asking what students would be doing differently when they move one number closer to their goal. Because taking small steps increases the chance of reaching the eventual goals, you should help the student identify 10% gains that are realistically achievable. All the preceding steps—identifying goals in the positive, exploring the miracle question and hypothetical solutions, and identifying exceptions to problems and instances of success—prepare students to think in terms of solutions. Envisioning further success becomes easier.

To encourage further progress, ask students presuppositional questions such as these: "What are you going to be doing when you move up one number on the scale?" "When you move up 10% on the scale, what will your teachers (parents, siblings) see you doing that will show them this is happening?" "What will I see you do when I see that you have moved from a 4 to a 5?" Questions asked this way (using "when rather than if") send a positive message by assuming that progress will happen. The answers to these questions are explored by detailing how students will make these changes happen for themselves.

FLAGGING THE MINEFIELD: IDENTIFYING AND OVERCOMING OBSTACLES TO SUCCESS

After students have identified how they can advance 10% toward their goals, familiarizing clients with obstacles prepares them for the challenge that lies ahead. Students and counselors identify (flag) barriers (mines) to accomplishing goals. This helps students to be realistic about the hard work before them. Anticipating mines and flagging where they may occur prevent students from being caught off guard and discouraged.

Flagging the minefield is designed to help students identify ways they might address obstacles. One approach is to review strategies students previously have used with success in dealing with barriers. You can initiate this discussion with comments such as these:

- "Your plan sounds great. However, we both know that sometimes, something or some people may get in the way of your accomplishing what you intend to do. How do you think that could happen in your situation?"
- "When that has happened in the past, what have you done that has worked to keep you on track?"
- "What do you think you can do to not let these things get in your way?"

CONCLUDING THE INITIAL SESSION WITH A MESSAGE

SFBC, as originally developed, used a team approach. While the counselors work with clients, others on the team observe behind one-way glass and periodically phone the counselors to share suggestions. At the conclusion of the session, counselors excuse themselves to consult with the team to process the session and prepare a message for the client(s). The message consists of three parts: (a) compliments, (b) a bridging statement, and (c) a task.

Although this procedure may at first seem strange and unnecessary, it has benefits. This strategy gives counselors a few minutes to process what occurred in the meeting, communicates to clients that the counselors are giving careful thought to the session, and provides counselors time to review their notes and consult with the team to construct a message that will best help their clients. However, as a school counselor, you do not typically have the resources to work on teams. Instead, use this time at the end of the session as a quiet time to reflect on the session and to write a message. There are some practical tips for making this reflection time comfortable for students as well as productive for you as the counselor.

In most cases, you will leave the room to reflect and write the message, but there are some alternatives. You can give students a written assignment to be completed while you construct the message. For example, you may ask students to draw a picture of what their miracle would look like, or make a sketch or describe in a note what they learned in today's session or what they would see themselves doing to show they are on track for making things better. The following is an example of a note written by a 15-year-old high school freshman to a counseling practicum student at the conclusion of the final SFBC session.

Lisa,

Through the time that I have seen you, you have enabled me to speak my mind, realize my good points and mostly turn my life around. Thank you for helping me realize all the success I have accomplished. In such a short period of time, my life has changed so greatly. I think I noticed mostly that if I want respect, I have to give it. I never thought of it until I came to you. I think from just those sessions that we had, my whole life will never be the same. Now I have a more open mind and with your help I know I can succeed in anything, I just have to try. Not a lot of effort has been given by me before, but now I give it all. Mentally, I have changed and I have succeeded in the goal that I set at the beginning of our sessions, so again, I greatly appreciate everything.

Brooke

Messages are a critical part of the SFBC process. They serve as a positive reinforcement for what has occurred in the interview by reminding students of their resources and strengths and providing a homework assignment that enables students to keep on track toward accomplishing their goals.

Note Taking

During the meeting, you should take notes on information that can be used to compliment students. To construct a message, compliments are drawn from goal statements, responses to the miracle question, instances of success or exceptions to problems, and scaling responses. When students observe you only noting positives, successes, strengths, and resources, students feel reinforced to continue what is working for them. I have noticed that students may even remind you to note something positive you may not have written down. Note taking can be distracting. To minimize distraction by reducing writing time, I have found it helps to use a note sheet (prepared by a former student, Kim McKinney), that lists the steps of the model and provides space to write notes related to each step (see Figure 4.2 in Chapter 4).

If you plan to leave your office to construct a message, this procedure is best introduced at the beginning of the initial interview so that students will not be surprised when you announce that you need a few minutes to think about the meeting, look over your notes, and construct a message. This is a typical way to introduce the message-writing phase:

> Well, I have run out of questions. Do you have any questions for me? Are there any other things I need to know to help you? If not, I need to take a few minutes to think about everything that you have said and review my notes so I can write you a message you can take with you. While I'm gone, you may want to think about what was the most helpful part of our meeting and why you think this.

With elementary school–aged children, it works well to remain with them while writing the message. As mentioned earlier, I have found that asking them to draw a picture of what their miracle would look like helps them review what they learned in the session. Before reading the message, you and the student can discuss the picture, which also reveals the session's impact on the child. The example shown in Figure 3.1 of a picture drawn by a 10-year-old elementary school student shows how she was able to "click on" more pleasant thoughts, such as taking part in sports, riding her bike, and playing games, rather than obsessing about her mother's health, which had interfered with doing her schoolwork and enjoying herself at home.

After you read the message, give the student a copy and retain one for your files. Because messages are all positive, citing students' strengths and attributes, most students are willing to share their notes with significant others. When students show off their messages to their parents and teachers, the parents and

Figure 3.1   An Elementary School Student's Drawing of Her Miracle

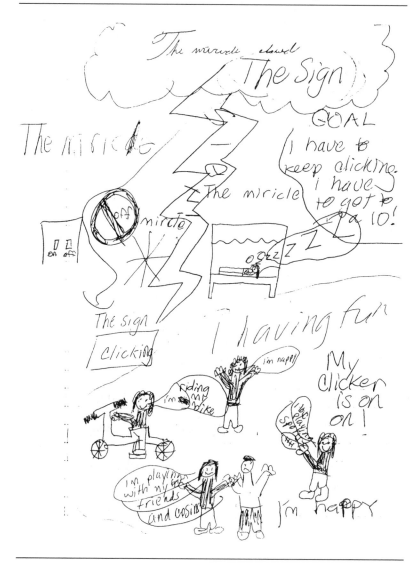

teachers are exposed to positive aspects of their children and students they may have overlooked. The message not only reinforces students' successes but also helps others recognize strengths in students as well.

Compliments

Throughout each session, listen carefully for strengths, solutions, and what is working—even if just a little—and look for times when things are not quite as bad as at other times. Compliments are drawn from your notes about all the student's successes along with the concrete details associated with each accomplishment. Each message should include at least three compliments, each referring to specific behaviors exhibited by the student. Compliments are like seeds that can be cultivated later when the task is assigned at the end of the message. The following are among the characteristics students display that can serve as the basis for compliments. Keep in mind that many of these phrases are interchangeable. For example, both thoughts and decisions can be growth producing or healthy.

- Actions that indicate courage, healthy risk taking, compromise, or follow-through
- Efforts that demonstrate strength, a challenge, growth, or planning
- Commitments that show loyalty, effort, dedication, or devotion
- Attitudes that reflect tolerance, acceptance, flexibility, common sense, or helpfulness
- Thoughts that are creative, positive, rational, sensitive, or insightful
- Desires that are realistic, healthy, sensible, or growth producing
- Decisions that are based on judgment, consequences, opportunities, or options
- Attributes of being mature, smart, understanding, empathetic, or cooperative

The following compliments were part of a message presented to a sixth-grade boy who wanted to pass to the seventh grade but was failing in school.

The Message:

I'm really impressed with the commitment you have to do better in school. Your improvement in your grades this last week shows that you are capable of doing well in school.

Getting an A and a B on recent tests proves that you really want to do better, and you know how to make it happen for yourself by studying 30 minutes each night and going to bed by 10 P.M.

Your desire to feel better about yourself by getting better grades tells me that you really care about yourself, your mom, your teachers, and your friends. You also recognize that it's important to pass so you can be with the kids your own age next year, and your recent grades demonstrate that you are smart and you can be successful.

The compliments in this message reflected back the student's own words in the interview to reinforce specific behaviors that were on track toward achieving his goal.

Bridging Statements

A bridging statement connects the compliment and task portions of the message. First, the compliments set the stage by identifying solutions. Then, based on these solutions, the bridge provides a rationale for a task that will be assigned. A bridge consists of two parts: (a) a brief reference to what the student wants (the goal) as a result of counseling and (b) a short statement intended to initiate the task. Examples of this include the following:

- Because of your efforts (desires) to (improve your grades), I would urge you to . . .
- To help you remain focused on (getting to school on time), it would be in your best interest to . . .
- To keep you going on the path to (remaining calm when your dad yells at you), I would suggest . . .
- Because you realize (recognize, understand) the benefits of (making friends), it would be helpful to . . .
- As a result of your commitment to (attend school instead of doing drugs), you may want to . . .

In the situation mentioned previously with the student who wanted to pass to the seventh grade, the compliments were followed by this bridging statement: "Because of your desire to do better in school and feel better about yourself as well, I would suggest that you . . ." Bridging statements are natural links connecting goals and solutions to homework tasks.

Tasks

The third part of the message is the task or homework assignment. Contrary to other theoretical approaches, the assignment is nonspecific. Throughout counseling, you have conveyed confidence in your students' abilities to name their own goals and identify what life would be like if they were reaching their goals. You have underscored your clients' abilities to bring about instances of success that have helped them progress. Essentially, the interview translates into a boost to self-esteem that demonstrates your faith in the student's ability to succeed. The assignment of nonspecific tasks conveys the clear signal that students are trusted to complete the homework in ways that work best for them. Being nonspecific also encourages students' creativity. If you are concerned that your students may get stuck in following through with a nonspecific task, it helps to recognize that the compliment portion of the message spells out the details of students' successes and promotes a plan of action.

The following tasks exemplify the types of assignments that work with these circumstances:

- When students can identify instances of success or exceptions to problems, assign them to (a) do more of the behaviors that brought them success or exceptions, (b) notice and continue to do what has been working for them, or (c) do what it takes to move up one number on their scale of 0–10.
- When students are unclear about their goals or are reluctant to take action or focus on their problems, assign them to (a) observe the times when things are better, (b) notice when exceptions are happening, (c) pay attention to when the problem is less intense, (d) notice what they are doing when they are moving in the right direction, or (e) pretend that their miracle is happening for one day.
- When students don't recognize a problem or can't come up with a goal for counseling, compliment them for positives and successes, but do not assign a task.

In the previous example of the student who was failing but wanted to pass, the following task was assigned: "Notice between now and next week, when we meet again, the times you have been successful in doing your homework, especially how you keep yourself on track when you're tempted to get sidetracked."

For Sue's case, cited earlier, the following section shows the counselor's interview with Sue and the accompanying message prepared for her.

Goal:

I want to be honest with my mother.

I want to improve my relationship with my mother.

I want to avoid doing things I know are wrong that my friends ask me to do.

Miracle:

Mom would say, "I trust you, you can go out with your friends."

Be truthful with Mom because I don't want to hurt her.

My attitude would change, I would cooperate, I would say, "Okay, that's fine."

Spend more time on weekends with Mom, watch TV together, share moments.

Accept her answers, "Okay, if it will feel better for you I'll do something else."

Attitude would be better, "I would look her in the eyes without rolling mine."

Say "Hi" to everyone in the family in the morning.

Feed the cat and the animals.

Fold the towels and volunteer to help Mom.

Instances/exceptions:

While playing Nintendo, I fed the cat when asked.

Got the dirty clothes when told to get them.

Scaling:

At 3 because I had a talk with Mom on Sunday.

I helped out doing things around the house.

Coming in to see you for counseling.

What will you be doing when you are at a 4 that you're not doing now?

I need to do more things for Mom, i.e., volunteer to clean the birdcage.

Fold towels, clean up the living room before Mom gets home from work.

Continue to see the counselor.

Talk to Mom and be truthful with her.

From these notes, the following message was constructed:

Compliment

I am impressed with how much you want to establish a trusting and honest relationship with your mom by acting in responsible ways. Making comments to your mom like, "OK, that's fine" or "OK, I will do something else" will prove to her that you can be cooperative.

You recognize that making direct eye contact instead of rolling your eyes, saying hello to family members, helping around the house by feeding the animals, and doing some of the laundry and other household chores will demonstrate to your mom that your attitude has improved.

You also realize that seeking counseling help, having honest talks with your mom and cleaning the house before she gets home from work will do much to make things better between you and her. You have already begun to show improvement by feeding the cat and getting the dirty clothes when asked.

You recognize that changing your attitude by being more cooperative, accepting what she says rather than arguing, and spending more time with her can lead to a more positive relationship, and you want that very much. You also realize what you have to do to begin to make things better at home (be more friendly by saying hello to family members, help out with the animals, and volunteer to do things around the house), and you have already begun these things.

Bridge

Because of your commitment to make things better at home,

Task

I would suggest you continue to do those things that you have just started that are working for you and notice what you are doing to move up the scale one notch to a 4.

SUMMARY

Through rediscovering unrecognized solutions and exceptions, students are empowered to pursue their goals. Scaling techniques offer methods to assess how far students have come and what they need to do to be even more successful. The meeting concludes by giving a message that indicates compliments and homework tasks that are constructed from the counselor's notes to reinforce the student's continued efforts to improve. Chapter 4 presents an entire SFBC session demonstrating the components addressed in this and the previous chapter.

PRACTICE EXERCISE

From the previous exercise in Chapter 2, bring to mind the answers you gave to the miracle question and subsequent questions. Those responses will help you identify solutions when answering the following queries.

- Recall a time when some of your miracle occurred, even in just a small way—perhaps some instance when things weren't quite as bad or when things were a little bit better.

  What was different about you this time?

  Who else noticed this change in you this time?

  How did they respond when they observed you act this way?

- Recall other instances when a part of your miracle has happened.

  How do you account for it happening then?

- On a scale ranging from 0–10, with 0 being the worst you could imagine your problem could ever be and 10 being the day after your miracle happened, where would you place yourself on that scale now?

  What have you done to get from a 0 to the place you are now?

  What are you going to be doing when you move up 10% on your scale?

  What will keep you going when something comes up that will impede your progress?

CHAPTER FOUR

Connecting
the Pieces

T he previous chapters have described components of the
initial interview of SFBC. The next step involves putting
all of the components together and conceptualizing how to implement the model. This chapter opens with a brief review and road
map of all the steps, followed by an actual case that demonstrates
the solution-focused approach with a student. The case has itali-
cized notes interspersed in the dialogue to highlight the stages
in the process. As you review the dialogue, you are encouraged
to take notes and use these notes to prepare a message for the
student in the case. You can compare the message you've prepared
with the one actually given to the student.

COMPONENTS OF THE FIRST SESSION

This section draws from previous descriptions and examples to
review the components of the first session, step by step.

1. What's the Reason You Have
Come to See Me? What's Your Goal?

Acknowledge by listening and reflecting the students' concerns. Use responses that indicate your understanding, such as "I
see," "Uh huh," "Sounds like a tough situation," head nods, and

empathetic comments that show students that you are with them. Let students get their problems off their chests. Then ask what they want to accomplish from counseling—their goal. Try to establish a goal in positive terms (something they will be doing rather than the absence of some behavior).

2. The Miracle Question

This is not a goal but a means to establish a goal. It prompts students to fantasize or identify a "solution picture" of what life would be like without the problem. Asking this type of question helps clients envision possibilities that may be available but have gone unrecognized. Examples include the following:

- "Suppose tonight after you go to sleep a miracle occurs, and because you are sleeping you don't know it happens. The miracle solves the problem that brought you here. When you wake up in the morning, what clues are you going to see that will lead you to discover that this miracle has happened?"
- "If I waved a magic wand over your head that would get rid of your problem right now, what would you notice that would be different in your life?"
- "Picture yourself a year from now, after we have worked together and successfully settled your problem. What will you notice will be different in your life that will tell you we no longer need to meet?"

The student's answers to these types of questions may not be behaviorally specific, or they may indicate an emotion or a miracle that is impossible. When this occurs, it is important to clarify a detailed picture of what students will be *doing* when the miracle happens. Ask the client, "What else will you notice after this miracle?" Ask this three or four times. Use this question to help expand the options clients will see as possible.

It also helps to use questions that elicit observations by significant others, such as the following:

- "What would your (teacher, friend, sibling, mom, dad, etc.) notice you would be doing differently after this miracle?"

3. First Sign

These supportive follow-up questions cause students to begin thinking about the first small steps to make their goals a reality.

- "What will be the first small sign that you will notice that will tell you that this miracle is beginning to happen?"
- "Who will be the first to see that this miracle is happening? What will they see?"
- "When you are no longer (losing your temper, starting arguments, etc.), what would have been the first thing you would have noticed that you did that was different and would tell us that you're on the right road to make your miracle happen?"
- "If I were a fly on the wall and I saw that you had solved your problem, what would I have seen (heard) you doing that would tell me that you were on track to starting to resolve what led you to come to see me?"

4. Instances/Exceptions

Have students identify their resources—the times when they are already exhibiting behaviors related to their goals. Instances often are generated from students' responses to the miracle and "what else" questions. Use statements based on the assumption that the miracle has already happened as a way to help students think of instances of success and exceptions to their problems.

- "Tell me about the times when some of this miracle has already happened—even just a little bit."

As students recall the instances in their lives when the problem didn't exist, discovering the details of how they avoided the problem provides a road map for solutions, success, and empowerment.

- "Tell me about when you have been a little less sad. What was different about that time? What did you do to make that happen for yourself?"
- "Tell me about the time when you were tempted not to do your schoolwork but did it anyway. How did you manage to pull that off?"
- "How close have you come to this miracle recently?"

In response to their explanations, cheerlead or compliment clients for their effective actions or thoughts.

- "Really! You did that even though you were under all that pressure? That's amazing because it would have been easy to give up and you didn't."
- "That's unbelievable—that you could remain calm under those circumstances. Most people would have lost it, but you didn't. How were you able to do that?"

5. Scaling 0–10

Asking students to rate their current status not only establishes a baseline for measuring growth but also determines how they have arrived at where they are and what they can to do to move up the scale.

- "On a scale from 0–10, with 0 being the worst your situation has ever been and 10 being after your miracle has happened to its fullest extent, where do you think you are now?"

Follow up with questions that ascertain what they have done to reach their present rating. Generally students rate themselves as being higher than their lowest point, and discovering what they have done to cause this is motivating. Cheerleading is effective here, along with helping students identify the details of their success.

- "Is that right, you are at a 3? What have you done that has enabled you to get to a 3?"

To help students progress up the scale and accomplish small, attainable goals, ask them to identify the things they will need to do to advance one point on the scale.

- "What will you be doing differently when you get yourself to a 4? How will you make that happen?"

Sometimes identifying possible obstacles to their goal (flagging the minefield) is also productive here.

- "Even though you know what to do to avoid talking to your buddies in class when the teacher is speaking, how are you going to handle it when your friends start to talk to you?"

6. The Message

Before writing the message, find out if any other information would be pertinent for you to know and answer any questions the client may have. At this point in the process, clients seldom have additional information or questions.

- "Is there anything else I should know or any questions that you have before I take a few minutes to put my thoughts together about our meeting and come back to you with a message?"

This step involves composing a note to the student that reflects compliments as well as a bridging statement that provides a rationale for the task the student is assigned to accomplish before the next session.

Beginning counselors have found several tools to be useful in taking notes and staying on track in the SFBC sequence—a "road map" to SFBC and a specially prepared note sheet. The road map provides a quick reference guide to the sequence of steps in the first session of the SFBC model (see Figure 4.1 for the Session 1 Road Map to Solutions). The Note Sheet for Session 1 (Figure 4.2) is specially designed to help you organize your notes for each step of the sequence. I recommend using these tools together. Make a full-size photocopy of the road map and the note sheet for the first session and place the road map on the left side of a bifold notepad or binder and place the note sheet on the right side. This gives you convenient access to both tools during the session.

CASE STUDY WITH PEDRO: SESSION ONE

As you read this case, you may want to take notes so you can practice constructing a message. Then you can compare your message with the one presented at the end of this chapter. This case involves Pedro, a 12-year-old, sixth-grade boy sent to me because of

Figure 4.1   Session 1 Road Map to Solutions

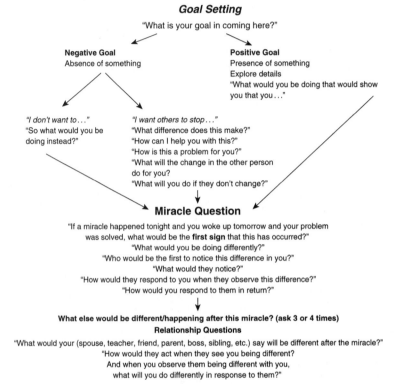

Explain Note Taking and Message

Goal Setting
"What is your goal in coming here?"

Negative Goal
Absence of something

Positive Goal
Presence of something
Explore details
"What would you be doing that would show you that you..."

"I don't want to..."
"So what would you be doing instead?"

"I want others to stop..."
"What difference does this make?"
"How can I help you with this?"
"How is this a problem for you?"
"What will the change in the other person do for you?
"What will you do if they don't change?"

Miracle Question
"If a miracle happened tonight and you woke up tomorrow and your problem was solved, what would be the **first sign** that this has occurred?"
"What would you be doing differently?"
"Who would be the first to notice this difference in you?"
"What would they notice?"
"How would they respond to you when they observe this difference?"
"How would you respond to them in return?"

↓

What else would be different/happening after this miracle? (ask 3 or 4 times)
Relationship Questions
"What would your (spouse, teacher, friend, parent, boss, sibling, etc.) say will be different after the miracle?"
"How would they act when they see you being different?
And when you observe them being different with you,
what will you do differently in response to them?"

Instances/Exceptions
"**Tell me** when some of this miracle 'is happening' or has already happened even just a little bit?"
(Cheerlead)

↓

Scaling
"On a scale of 0–10, where 0 is when things were the worst they could be and where 10 is the day after the miracle, where are you right now?" **(Cheerlead)**
"When you're 10% higher, what will you be doing differently?"
(Flag the minefield) "What will you do if...?"

↓

Anything Else I Need to Ask/Know?

↓

Message
Compliments (At Least 3) – Bridge – Task

Figure 4.2   SFBC Note Sheet for Session 1

Client: _____

Date: _____   **Date & Time of Next Session:** _____

CLIENT'S GOAL: • State in positive terms. • Define by behavioral actions.	
MIRACLE QUESTION: If a miracle happened tonight, and you woke up tomorrow and your problem was solved, what would be the first sign that this has occurred? • What would you be doing differently? • What else would be different after the miracle? **Relationship Questions:** RIPPLE EFFECT • Who would notice the change in you? • What would they notice? • How would they respond to you? • How would you then respond to them? **Repeat sequence of relationship questions 3 or 4 times**	
INSTANCES/ EXCEPTIONS: • When has this miracle already happened, even just a little bit? • How were *you* able to make this happen? (Help student take ownership and then cheerlead.)	
SCALING: • On a scale of 0–10, with 0 being the worst and 10 being the best, where would you rate yourself today? • How did you get to a ____ today? • When you move one number higher, what will you see yourself doing? ****Flag the minefield:** What will you do if . . . ?	0 1 2 3 4 5 6 7 8 9 10
UNFINISHED BUSINESS: Is there anything else I need to know?	
MESSAGE: • Compliments (3): about current successes. • Bridge: to connect the goal and the task. • Task: general actions or observations client is to carry out.	

frequent suspensions from school. The student provides additional background in the course of the interview that follows. The opening explanation of the process has been deleted to avoid repeating previous information (C = Counselor; P = Pedro).

C: What did you come to see me about?

P: I guess my attitude and behavior.

C: What do you mean, "attitude and behavior"?

P: Sometimes, when I raise my hand first and teacher calls on somebody else, I get mad 'cause I raised my hand first. When some of the teachers tell me to do something, I don't do it. I just get an attitude about it, and I don't follow directions.

(Identifying the goal)

C: So, what would you like to be able to do as a result of our meetings?

P: I guess learn to do what I'm told.

C: Sounds like you really mean that.

P: When I raise my hand first and the teacher sees me and they call on somebody else, I get mad; I get mad.

C: And when you get mad, what do you do?

P: Throw a fit.

C: And what does that look like?

P: I would just start mumbling and stuff, mumbling out words and disturbing the class. I want to stop doing that.

(Reframing from the absence of something to the presence of something)

C: So, what would you like to do rather than throw a fit?

P: Just put my hand down or just hold my hand up and just wait till she calls on me. Instead of throwing a fit, I just raise my hand up until she calls on me.

C: Just keep your hand up.

P: Or just let my hand down.

(Detailing specific behaviors)

C: So, you would like to leave your hand up until she does call on you or just put your hand down. What would you be doing or what would you be thinking when you aren't getting called on?

P: Just leave it down and if I know the answer, just write the answer on my paper instead of throwing a fit. Just write my answer down.

(Cheerleading)

C: Hey, that's pretty clever. So, you would just be kind of checking yourself out by writing it down to see if you got it right.

P: Yeah.

C: How did you come up with that idea?

P: I just came up with it.

(Cheerleading)

C: That's pretty creative, you know. Did you know that you are creative?

P: Sometimes.

(Hypothetical miracle question)

C: I have a strange question to ask that may be hard to answer. Suppose that when you went to sleep tonight and because you were sleeping you didn't know this was happening, but a miracle occurred. When you woke up the next morning, all your problems were solved. Gone, just disappeared. And when you woke up, you said to yourself, "Something happened during the night because all of my problems are gone. My attitude, my behavior— those problems have all just disappeared." What would you notice that was different when you woke up that would tell you that this miracle happened?

P: When I get to school, I won't have an attitude.

(Reframing from the absence of something to the presence of something)

C: Okay, so the attitude would be gone. When it's gone, what would be in place of it? Because it disappeared, something has got to happen to take its place. What would take the place of that attitude?

P: My education.

C: What do you mean by that?

P: My work—I'd be more on my work than on my attitude.

(Detailing specific behaviors)

C: How would you know you were on your work? How would your teacher know you were on your work? What would your teacher see you doing?

P: I would be looking in the book. She'd be looking at me, and I'd have my eyes on the book instead of talking to people.

(Question that exposes reciprocal effects)

C: Okay, so your eyes would be looking at the book, you wouldn't be talking to people, you'd be looking at your book. And if that happened, how do you think your teachers would treat you when they saw you do that?

P: They would probably be nicer to me and call on me more when I raise my hand.

C: And if that were to happen, what would you do?

P: I would do what they tell me to do.

(What else question)

C: It sounds like you all would get along better. What else do you think might be going on when the attitude is gone? There would be something else in its place. What else do you see yourself doing?

P: I don't know.

C: If you did know? That's a tough question—a hard, hard question I'm asking you. Some of the questions I'll ask you are going to be real tough to answer. This is one of them.

P: I'd be behaving, I guess.

(Detailing specific behaviors)

C: You'd be behaving. What would that look like? If I were sitting inside your classroom, and I were seeing you behaving, what would I see you doing?

P: Getting my work on the board. What we're supposed to do is on the board. As soon as I get in class, I'd sit in my seat, write in my agenda. Then put my agenda up, get some paper out, and be ready to work.

C: Okay, so you would be sitting in your seat and writing out an agenda.

P: Yeah. Write out what we're going to do that's on the board, that's what I write in my agenda.

C: Okay, so you would see what's on the agenda for the day, and you would write it in your agenda book.

P: Yeah. The agenda has what the date is and what our assignment is for that day.

(Question that exposes reciprocal effects)

C: Tell me then, if you were behaving and doing your work as you just described, what would your teachers do in return?

P: They would probably be saying "Good, good job, Pedro," about me for doing better, and my grades would go up.

C: So, if your teachers were like that with you, how do you think you would respond to them?

P: I would be smiling and work harder to get my grades up.

C: And, when they see you smiling and putting in more effort, how would your teachers act toward you?

P: They would be real happy and would trust me more, and I'd like that.

(What else question)

C: Okay, so what else do you think you would notice that would tell you that a miracle has happened and that your attitude is gone?

P: I'd sit up in my seat.

C: Okay, you'd sit up in your seat—instead of slouching, you mean?

P: Yeah. I won't be chewing gum. No candy.

C: No gum or candy. So, your mouth would be empty?

P: Yeah. When I go to the restroom, I won't be roaming the halls.

C: Okay, so you'd just go straight to the restroom and back.

P: Yeah.

(Question that exposes reciprocal effects)

C: How do you think your teachers would respond to seeing you doing these things?

P: They would like it.

C: So, what do you think they would do?

P: They would smile and say nice things about me.

C: And how would you respond to them when they say nice things about you?

P: I'd probably say "thank you" and work even harder.

(What else question)

C: What else would happen?

P: I won't be tardy, late to class.

(Reframing from the absence of something to the presence of something)

C: So, instead of being tardy or late to class, what would you be doing?

P: I'd go to class on time.

C: How would you make that happen?

P: I would go straight from one class to the next without making any stops with all my books.

C: What would you do with those books? You mean get them all together?

P: Yeah. Carry all your books, so you can have them for each class.

C: Okay. Get all the books for each class?

P: Yeah. And have all your folders for your classes. You're supposed to have your folder with paper in the clip for each class so you can do your work.

C: Okay, so be organized so that you can do your work and have all your work in your folders. Gosh, you know a bunch. How do you know all this stuff?

P: That's what we're supposed to do.

(Cheerleading)

C: Yeah, but most kids don't remember all that kind of stuff. How do you remember all that?

P: They told us at the beginning of the school year you have to have all your folders. Like for science, you're supposed to have a purple folder, language arts is red, reading is black, and social studies is green. You are supposed to put those subjects on your folder and write your name at the top so that they will know whose folder it is. And your work is supposed to be in the folder so you won't lose your work and it won't be all over the place. And you are supposed to carry your agenda and your book with you.

C: And you remembered all that?

P: Yeah.

C: Yeah, but most kids would forget all those details, and you remembered it all. That's neat that you can remember all that. That says something to me about how you can think. You've got a good memory.

P: I don't have . . . Yeah, I guess I do have a good memory. Kind of got a good memory.

(Cheerleading and a what else question)

C: Well, you sure remembered that well. You remembered all the things that they said you have to have. You have to have paper in your folders; you have to have an agenda. It sounds to me like you know what to do. Wow! What else, Pedro, would tell you that this miracle has happened?

P: I'd be getting A's and B's on my report card instead of getting them bad grades, and I'd get to go on field trips.

(Detailing specific behaviors)

C: You'd be getting A's and B's and going on the field trips that you don't go on now. What other things would you be doing that would tell you that you were on the path to getting A's and B's on your report card?

P: I would do my homework right after school before I go out with my friends and then I would be put on the Honors Team.

(First sign of miracle question)

C: Here is another tough question. What would be the first sign for you that this miracle has happened? What would tell you? How would you know that gosh, maybe this miracle is happening to me even if it was just a little bit. What is the first thing that you would notice?

P: The first thing I'd notice is I'd be getting A's and B's on my report card, and the teachers would be saying, "Good job, Pedro, you are doing your work." And I would ask them, "Have I turned in all my work?" And they would say, "Yes."

C: So, the first sign is, teachers would say, "Good job, Pedro." And you'd be getting better grades.

P: That's right.

C: Who else would notice this change in you?

P: My mother would notice.

C: What would she see you doing that would tell her that you're different?

P: I wouldn't be watching as much TV and arguing with my cousin.

(Reframing from the absence of something to the presence of something)

C: So, if you weren't watching TV and arguing, what would you be doing instead?

P: I would be doing my homework in my room with the door locked so nobody could bother me.

(What else question)

C: What other things would you notice?

P: People getting to like me.

(Question that exposes reciprocal effects)

C: How would you know that?

P: Like if I showed them my report card, they would say, "Dang, Pedro. You got all A's and B's. How did you get all them A's and B's? Your mama is going to be proud of you."

C: Oh. Mom would be proud too. Would you like that?

P: Yeah.

C: How would Mom show you she was proud? How would you know my mom's really proud of me? What would tell you that Mom is proud of you?

P: She's going to show everybody my report card.

C: She's going to show you off, huh? What else would she do that would tell that she is proud?

P: She'd buy me something.

(Instances/exceptions questions)

C: I have another tough question for you. Tell me about some times when some of these things are happening already, if even just a little bit?

P: Today some of these things have happened.

C: Is that right? Tell me about today.

P: Well, my attitude is changing.

C: Is that right? Tell me how.

P: I didn't throw no fit to no teachers. When my teacher told me to come down here, she told me to make sure to get all my work ready so I can do it, and I said, "Okay."

C: Usually, you would have thrown a fit?

P: Yeah.

(Cheerleading and detailing specific behaviors)

C: That's amazing! How did you do that?

P: I just did it 'cause my mom said. She wrote me a note this morning before she left for work, and she said for me to listen to what them teachers tell you. Listen to what they tell you to do and do it.

C: So, you think that's what did it for you?

P: Yeah.

   (Accepting ownership statement)

C: But I've got to tell you something. I have an idea that your mother has written notes like that to you before, hasn't she?

P: Yeah.

C: And you still didn't do what she asked you to do.

P: Yeah.

C: But you did it today.

P: Yeah.

C: You did it today. So, that may have helped you some. But it must have been something that you did, something you did for you to make that happen.

P: Ms. Smith talked to me. I had to have a conference with Ms. Smith. She told me you don't get an education without following directions.

C: So, you listened to Ms. Smith and it made some sense to you?

P: Yeah.

C: I bet you've had those lectures before, though, haven't you?

P: Yeah.

   (Accepting ownership statement and mindmapping solutions)

C: And it didn't work.

P: No.

C: So, what made it work today? What made that different today for you?

P: I don't want to be suspended no more.

C: That sounds like a change for you. You don't want to get suspended?

P: Yeah.

C: And when you're saying that, it sounds like you are saying, "I'm too important to let that happen to me." How do you account for that change? For you saying, "Hey, I don't want to get suspended." What's going on in you that made that change in you?

P: Everybody being proud of me that I haven't got suspended for a few days.

C: So, people are proud of you. You kind of like the way people see you as "Hey, I'm taking charge of myself. I don't have to get suspended. I can behave if I want to."

P: Yeah.

C: Hmm. That's neat. How have you managed to do that for yourself? To make yourself say, "People are proud of me and I don't want to get suspended no more. I want to be here at school." How did you do that?

P: I just said, "I can do it."

C: So, you told yourself, "I can do it."

P: Yeah.

  (Mindmapping)

C: My guess is, you have probably told yourself that before, haven't you?

P: Yeah.

C: But this is different. What made it different this time?

P: My mother told me. My grandmother and my granddaddy told me they were proud of me.

C: So, it sounds to me like you really respect and want to please them too.

P: Yeah.

C: So, this time, you are saying, I'm really going to do it.

P: Yeah.

  (Cheerleading)

C: Hmm. That's really super. That's fantastic that you are able to do that. That you respect and care enough about your mom and your grandparents—and yourself too. You care enough about yourself that you are going to keep yourself on track.

P: Yeah.

(Reviewing miracle to identify additional instances/exceptions)

C: Tell me about other times when some of the things are happening? Like, you are writing the things that are on the board, your eyes are on the book, you are sitting in your seat, you are going straight to the restroom and back, going to class on time, you are getting your books for each class. You have a folder in each class, you are getting better grades, you're going on field trips, you're on the Honors Team. Any of those kinds of things happening? Tell me about when some of those things are happening.

P: I have already been on the Honors Team before.

(Cheerleading)

C: Really! You have been on the Honors Team? Great! That's pretty hard to do?

P: Yeah.

C: What do you have to do to be on the Honors Team?

P: You have to have a good attitude. You have to have all your work turned in. Your behavior has got to be good and you have to get good grades.

C: You know, with all the difficulties you've had, you were on the Honors Team? How were you able to be on the Honors Team? How did you make that happen for yourself? What was different about that time when you were able to be on the Honors Team?

P: I did what they told me to do and just did my work. And then I just got put on the Honors Team.

(Cheerleading)

C: So, you can do it! Pedro can do it! If you want to, because you are smart enough to do that.

P: Yeah, I'm smart enough to do that. But see, when I'm around my friends, I'm talkative and stuff. I just talk to them too much when I'm around my friends. When I'm not around them, I just do my work and stuff.

C: Yeah, that's what you were saying before. You like to talk a lot with your friends, and that kind of takes over from doing the school stuff.

P: Yeah.

C: When you were on the Honors Team, I imagine that there were times when you could have talked to your friends, but you didn't.

P: Yeah, I wasn't talking as much then as I do now.

C: So, what you are saying is, you were able to control your talking to the point where you were able to be on the Honors Team and still be with your friends at the same time.

P: Yeah.

(Mindmapping solutions)

C: How did you figure out how to do that?

P: When I talked to my friends, I was at lunch, in the hallways, and in related arts class.

C: Oh I see. So, you figured out you can save your talk for the hallways and lunchtime and related arts. Did someone teach you that?

P: Yeah, they told me that talk was for the hallways, for lunch, and for related arts, instead of in the classroom, 'cause when you are in the classroom, you got work to do instead of talking.

C: So, what's it going to take for you to be able to do that again?

P: Just save my talking for the hallways and related arts instead of talking in class and just keep my eyes on my book and pull up my grades.

C: How are you going to manage to make that happen for yourself again?

P: Don't talk. Just don't talk at all in class. Only when the teacher asks me a question.

(Scaling)

C: Okay. Gosh, you seem to have the answers. You know the solutions. Let me ask you this question: On a scale from 0 to 10, with 0 being your attitude just stinks and your behavior is down at the bottom, to a 10 being your miracle has happened and all these things you described that you want to happen were going on for you—so you don't have any problem with your attitude or behavior at all. Where do you think you are right now, between 0 and 10?

P: I'm around a 5.

C: You're around a 5? That means you have already started to move in a positive direction toward a 10.

P: Yeah.

C: Now that's a big jump from a 0 to a 5. How have you managed to get yourself to a 5?

P: I've started now.

C: What have you started doing now?

P: Doing my work now instead of talking. Of my assignments, I only have three more problems to do.

C: So, when you are at a 6 what will you be doing then that you are not doing now?

P: I'm going to talk less. Get my work done, and when my work is done, then I can talk if the teacher says it's okay.

C: Okay, so you'd be finishing your work, then you will talk.

P: Yeah.

(Flagging the minefield)

C: Boy, I bet there's going to be some temptations, though, while you are doing your work, to start talking. What are you going to do when someone starts talking to you while you are still doing your work?

P: I'll just ignore them.

C: Hmm. Just like that. You can do that?

P: Yeah.

C: Really? That works?

P: Yeah. It works. Or I just tell them to leave me alone.

C: So, that would do it, getting to a 6—you want to finish your work first in class and that would tell you that you are on task.

P: Yeah.

C: I can't think of any other questions I need to ask you. Do you have any for me?

P: No.

C: Well then, I'm going to take a few minutes to think about what we talked about so I can write you the message we talked about at the beginning of our meeting today. While I'm gone, perhaps you might want to think about what helped you the most in our session.

SUMMARY

This chapter has presented a complete first interview demonstrating the application of the steps in SFBC. The case included prompts to assist you in associating process with content and provided an opportunity to practice taking notes in order to develop a message for the student. Messages include a task to be completed between sessions that will be addressed in a subsequent meeting. The next chapter discusses the components of second and subsequent interviews using the SFBC approach with students.

PRACTICE EXERCISE

Take a few minutes to write a message to Pedro. Then compare it with the following one.

Message

(Write out the message, photocopy it, read it out aloud to the student, and give a copy to the student to take home.)

Compliments

I'm really impressed with how smart you are, with your ability to know what it is you have to do to do better in school. I am really impressed with how much you care about improving your attitude and your behavior in school. Your efforts today by staying calm rather than throwing a fit with your teacher when she reminded you about your work demonstrate your ability to control yourself. I'm also amazed with your creativity in figuring out a way to at least let yourself know the answers to your teacher's questions even if you're not called on. Your thoughts about not wanting to be suspended show that you respect your mom, grandparents, and yourself a whole lot. Being on the Honors Team in September shows that you know what it takes to be successful, by doing your work and saving your talking time for the lunchroom, the halls, and in related arts and still being able to hang with your friends. You know what to do and how to do it.

Bridging Statement

Because of your desire to improve in school,

Task

I want you to notice the times things are better and what you are doing to move you up to a 6 this week.

ADDITIONAL EXERCISE

Appendix A contains the transcript of another complete first session of SFBC with prompts that will enable you to practice SFBC interventions. Then you can compare your interventions with the interventions I used with the student.

CHAPTER FIVE

Conducting Subsequent Sessions

S tudents returning for second or subsequent interviews already have been assigned to continue doing things that are working or to notice what's better in their lives. Follow-up meetings begin with the premise that students have continued this focus between interviews and have observed positive things that may have gone unrecognized otherwise. I have found that most students report positive changes, and those who report that no progress has occurred do, with further solution-focused exploration, identify at least minimal change. Some clients may not want to admit progress; however, because this approach emphasizes assets, students are more likely to acknowledge growth.

Following a well-organized process is just as important for subsequent sessions as it is for the first meeting. A sequence known as EARS guides the second and subsequent sessions (Berg, 1994). EARS is an acronym for

Elicit what's better;
Amplify the effects of what's better;
Reinforce how these changes were brought about; and
Start over again, discovering additional successes.

After using the EARS process to review instances of success or improvement, scaling is used to evaluate progress toward the student's goal in counseling. The student and counselor decide mutually whether additional counseling is needed. Second and subsequent interviews conclude with a message, just as in the first interview.

SUBSEQUENT SESSION COMPONENTS

Eliciting

To draw out the differences or positive changes that have occurred, ask, "What's better or different since the last time we met?" This resembles the initial session when you ask about instances of success or exceptions to problems as a way to explore overlooked resources.

Students may indicate that things are different but not necessarily better. As the differences are explored, pay careful attention to signs of any improvement even remotely connected to students' goals. As these successes are identified, the EARS process is initiated. Appropriate questions for this stage are similar to those used when exploring exceptions or instances of success in the first session. After clarifying the student's unrecognized success, next facilitate the amplifying, reinforcing, and starting over phases of the EARS method.

Some students will report that nothing is better or different. When this occurs, acknowledge students' comments while listening for even slight indications of things being better or not quite as bad as before. Inquiring about segments of time (e.g., the past several days, yesterday, today, or in the past hour) when things may have been a little better or not as bad helps students identify moments of success. The following leads are effective in facilitating this:

"Were things bad every minute of every day all week?"

"Tell me about the times that things were not quite as bad as other times."

"What was going on with you when things weren't quite as bad?"

"How were you different when it wasn't nearly as bad?"

"I'm guessing that if you think about that for a few minutes, you may be able to come up with something that was better or different."

"Perhaps if you thought about what may have happened just today, you may be able think of something to tell me."

"Who might have noticed something better or different with you since we last met?"

"What do you think they would have seen in you that would have told them some changes were going on with you?"

The following case example demonstrates reframing "nothing is different or better" responses into the recognition that things are in fact better (C = Counselor; S = Student).

C: What's better or different from when we saw each other last time?

S: Nothing, I had the same kind of week I usually have.

C: I have a hunch that during your usual week, there were some instances when things might have been a little better for you or maybe even not quite as bad.

S: I can't think of any.

C: Well, how about today, tell me about something that was better or different today!

S: Nothing really.

C: How about within the last hour before you came to see me?

S: You know, something was different last period in the lunchroom.

C: What was that?

S: They have this rule that you're not supposed to run in the lunchroom. Well, I ran in the lunchroom today, and the teacher told me to come back and walk, and I did.

C: Was that different for you?

S: Yeah.

C: How was it different?

S: I usually keep on running and get in trouble.

C: So, today was different for you, and it sounds like it's something that you said last week that you wanted to improve by following directions.

Through persistent questioning focused on specific segments of time, the counselor was able to elicit instances of success that had been unrecognized.

There may be times when students claim that things are actually worse than they reported in the previous meeting. When this surfaces, "listen for better" and also use interventions that help students recognize the coping skills that keep their situations from being even worse than they are. This builds on the assumption that things could be worse and that students are using their resources to keep things from deteriorating even further. Identifying how students are coping suggests solutions.

When students report things are declining, ask, "How come things aren't worse than they are?" Their answers help determine how they prevented things from completely falling apart. Capitalizing on instances of success in the midst of slippages can turn unpleasant experiences into moments of hope and triumph. Identifying some things that are better permits you to proceed with the EARS process.

Amplifying

The amplifying component of EARS investigates the ripple effect as changes in students' behaviors prompt change in others. Elaborating on the reciprocity evoked by their efforts empowers students to recognize the impact of their actions, which in turn reinforces students to take on further challenges that may not have been attempted otherwise. This component is similar to the reciprocal-relationship effect questions described in Chapter 2. At the close of the second counseling session, a fifth-grade boy in a behavior disorder class made the following comment that highlights the powerful impact of amplifying success:

> I like coming here because I don't get a chance to talk to anyone about all the good things I do and how my friends and teacher act with me when I do these good things. That helps me even do more good stuff.

Reinforcing

Reinforcing, or cheerleading, the third step in the sequence, is already familiar to most counselors. As students discover and are supported in their efforts to effect positive changes in their lives, mindmaps form to help them with future situations. Because this part of the interview resembles the instances/exceptions and cheerleading sections in Chapter 3, those techniques will not be reviewed again. The entire process is recycled again by *starting over* through eliciting what's better.

SCALING

After completing the EARS sequence, use previously described scaling techniques to evaluate students' progress since the past meeting. Counseling is not an exact science. The field has lacked a means to measure its effectiveness; however, scaling techniques provide a feasible means to gather repeated, self-reported measures of change. Typically you will find that students' ratings on a 0–10 scale will yield scores that reflect an upward, positive trend.

You should not remind students of their previous scores before asking them to rate where they are at the moment with their goal. Students need to respond as objectively as possible without being influenced by their earlier ratings.

Ratings That Show Improvement

To begin this aspect of subsequent sessions, ask students to estimate where they are, between 0 and 10, in reaching their goal. Apply the same procedures used with scaling described in

Chapter 3. Students are asked to identify what they have done to make progress, how others have reacted to them, and how they have managed to make this happen for themselves. Many of their responses to these queries will resemble interchanges that have already been described in the EARS sequence earlier in this chapter; therefore, these interventions are not described in detail again here. Acknowledging, supporting, and cheerleading are in order here. Soliciting details about students' progress on their scales may elicit new information revealing successes not previously mentioned. This presents another opportunity to process the components of successful efforts. As in their initial scaling in the first interview, ask students what they will be doing when they have moved up 10% on the scale. Flagging the minefield may also be used at this point in the interview.

Ratings That Indicate No Improvement or a Decline

Students may report they are at the same place or worse on their scale than they were in the previous session. When using the solution-focused approach, always keep in mind that instances of success or exceptions to problems are constantly occurring if we pay close attention. Even in the midst of times when things seem worse, there are moments when they are not quite as bad. And regardless of how bad things are, they could be worse. What students do to deintensify problems suggests they have coping skills. Helping clients recognize these skills also helps them identify solutions.

Scaling can be adapted to focus on other aspects of achieving goals as well. Asking students to rate from 0 to 10 their level of confidence that they will reach their goals is another scaling technique. You also can ask students how their teachers, parents, friends, or others would rate them on the scale to check how they sense that others perceive them.

ASSESSING THE NEED FOR FURTHER COUNSELING AND WRITING A MESSAGE

Before writing a message for a student, ask if the student is satisfied with what has been happening with counseling. If the student is not satisfied, explore what would help as a way to clarify the direction to be taken if further meetings are desired. Inquiries such as the following help students identify when it's time to stop counseling.

- How will you know you're done with counseling?
- What will you be doing on your own that will tell you that you don't need to see me anymore?
- When you have finished counseling, what will your teachers (parents) say you will be doing differently?
- How many more times do you think we need to meet until you're completely satisfied with counseling?
- Reaching what number on your scale will be enough for you to say you have been successful in here? So, how many more meetings will that take? (Keep in mind that estimates about the number of sessions can be amended as needed.)

After this issue is settled, construct a message as in the initial interview.

As with the first session, you can use a note sheet (developed by a former student, Kim McKinney) designed for the second and subsequent sessions to help in following the steps in the process, help organize your notes, and reduce writing time (see Figure 5.2).

A ROAD MAP AND NOTE SHEET FOR SECOND AND SUBSEQUENT SESSIONS

The road map (Figure 5.1) and note sheet (Figure 5.2) specially designed for second and subsequent sessions help serve as guides for the solution-focused sessions that follow the first meeting. I recommend using these tools together. Make a full-size photocopy of the road map and note sheet for second and subsequent sessions and place the road map on the left side of a bifold notepad or binder and place the note sheet on the right side. This gives you convenient access to both tools during the session.

Figure 5.1   Second and Subsequent Session Road Map

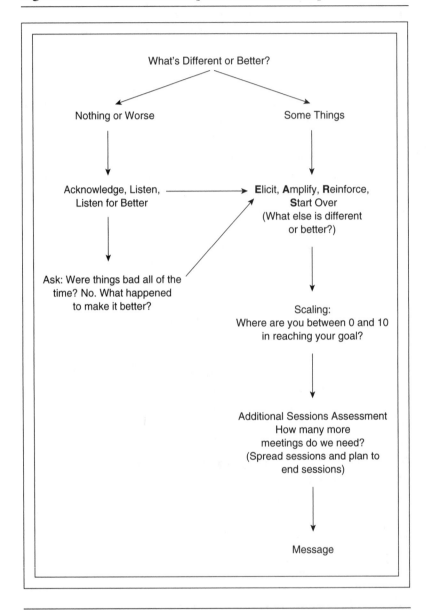

Figure 5.2 SFBC Note Sheet for Session 2 and Subsequent Sessions

Client: _____

Date: _____   Date & Time of Next Session: _____

CLIENT'S GOAL: • Identify the goal stated at the last session.	
ELICIT: • What is different or better since the last time we met? • Identify unrecognized successes. • How were you able to make this happen? **AMPLIFY:** • Who noticed the change in you? • What did they notice? • How did they respond to you? • How did you then respond to them? **REINFORCE:** • How did you make this change happen? • Cheerlead. **Repeat entire sequence 3 or 4 times:** What else was better?	
SCALING: • Where are you between 0 and 10 in reaching your goal? • How did you get to a __ today? • When you move one number higher, what will you see yourself doing? ****Flag the minefield:** What will you do if . . .?	0 1 2 3 4 5 6 7 8 9 10
ADDITIONAL SESSIONS: • Are you satisfied with our sessions? • How will you know when we no longer need to meet?	
MESSAGE: • Compliments (3): about current successes. • Bridge: to connect the goal and the task. • Task: general actions or observations the client is to carry out.	

SUBSEQUENT SESSIONS WITH PEDRO

The follow-up session 1 week later with Pedro, whose first session was presented in the previous chapter, demonstrates procedures for subsequent sessions. Pedro reported that things had been better since his first counseling appointment. He indicated that he was now going to every class on time, keeping his jacket in his locker, and beginning to do his work on entering his classes. He also reported that instead of roaming the halls, he would go straight back to class after going to the restroom. His grades and attitude about school had improved, and his teachers were now complimenting him on his progress. He also claimed that as a result of the changes he was making, he noticed that his teachers stopped picking on him and were nicer. This helped Pedro follow directions and comply with his teachers' requests.

When asked how he was able to make these changes happen, Pedro explained that he was able to remind himself that he didn't want any more referrals to the office and, if he cooperated with his teachers, his mother would no longer receive phone calls from school about his misbehaving. Moreover, he had decided to talk things through with other kids rather than hitting them. As a result, he got along better with them and with his teachers.

Pedro gave himself a rating of 9 with respect to his confidence that he would continue to improve. He reported that to achieve a 10, he would finish all his schoolwork in class before talking to his friends, continue to go to every class on time, do all of his work, and listen to his teachers.

The third meeting with Pedro was conducted 2 weeks after the second session. He reported he was listening to his teachers, turning in his schoolwork, going to class on time, talking only after doing his work with his teacher's permission, and avoiding fights by telling himself to forget about it. As a result of Pedro's continued improvement in school, he was put back on the Honors Team. Because Pedro decided he could continue to be successful on his own, no other sessions were to be scheduled unless he requested them. During the last 5 months of the school year, Pedro received only one referral to the office. Prior to counseling, he had weekly or biweekly referrals. His improved behavior continued throughout the summer and the following school year.

SUMMARY

The belief that students have the resources to make things better for themselves is the pervasive theme in subsequent SFBC sessions. Students are asked to identify improvements since the last meeting and the methods they have applied to create these positive changes. Scaling is used to measure growth and provide guidance for further progress. Meetings conclude by assessing the need for additional interviews and preparing and sharing the counselor's message. Follow-up sessions using the traditional solution-focused format are scheduled if needed.

CHAPTER SIX

Working With Reluctant and Mandated Students

Not all students who go to see a counselor do so willingly, and those referred to school administrators are generally sent for discipline reasons. This chapter will address how counselors and administrators may be able to convert reluctant students into willing counseling customers. In addition, this chapter will focus on how administrators can use the solution-focused approach as an alternative method for dealing with student discipline and suspension cases.

HELPING INVOLUNTARY CLIENTS BECOME CUSTOMERS TO THE PROCESS

Even after students identify why someone other than themselves wants them to receive help, they may not seem to be interested in counseling. However, asking questions focused on what they will get out of the experience turns many reluctant visitors into customers. When clients recognize that counseling may get the referring party "off their backs" or that disciplinary actions will cease, they generally become more receptive to establishing goals. You can use interventions such as the following to help students become more receptive: "Is what they want for you something you want as well, especially knowing that the hassles between the two of you would end?" "Would it be in your best interest to want these changes for yourself?" "If this happened even a little bit, what would it do for you and what effect would it have on you and . . . ?"

Case Study: Dealing With a Reluctant Client

The following case demonstrates how the counselor's persistence and patience eventually resulted in identification of positive goals, a first step in SFBC. Mike, an 11-year-old sixth-grader, was recently transferred from a small rural elementary school to a metropolitan middle school of more than 1,500 students. He was referred to the counselor but did not seem to know why and therefore had no goals for counseling (C = Counselor; M = Mike).

C: As a result of your coming here, what is going to be going on with you that will tell you that you don't need to come here anymore?

M: I don't know. I don't even know how I got sent here. For all I know, my mom just signed me up.

C: So, you think your mom signed you up?

M: Uh huh (nods yes).

C: What do you think would be the reason she would sign you up to come down here to see me?

M: I don't know why she would (shakes head no).

C: If you had to decide what you wanted to come down to see me for, what would it be?

M: I don't know why I have to come down here (puts head on hand, withdraws more).

C: So, that's a puzzle to you about what's the reason you're here. So, your mom hasn't had a discussion with you about this by saying to you, "Mike, I want you to go see a school counselor because I think you need, for some reason, to go there."

M: All I know is she signed me up for Extra School Studies, and then somebody asked my mom if she wanted me to talk to somebody.

C: What would you need to do Extra School Studies for?

M: 'Cause I'm failing.

C: You think that could be one of the reasons she wanted you to come and see me, to help you do better in school and pass your classes?

M: They said it was too late in the year to pass.

C: Would you like to pass if there's any way to pass?

M: *(Nods head strongly yes.)*

C: What would have to happen for you to pass?

M: Do all my work.

C: Is that something you would be interested in doing?

M: *(No response.)*

C: Maybe you're not real sure, but you're thinking about it?

M: *(No response; continues to look at floor.)*

C: Well, what do you think? By being here and meeting with me, passing would be your ultimate goal?

M: *(Nods head yes.)*

C: Is that what you'd like to have happen? It doesn't look real promising right now, but at least that would be something you would like to do?

M: *(Nods head yes.)*

C: At least, if you can't pass, we could at least go over the steps so it won't happen again. Is that something you might think about or want to work on?

M: Yeah.

C: So, am I hearing that you would like to develop some better habits? You didn't say that, but that's what I was getting from what you said.

M: Yeah, that would be good.

Taking the Student's Side

Another effective approach to involve reluctant clients is the "They're wrong, you're right" technique. By supporting students who claim the person who referred them for counseling is incorrect in his or her assessment, the counselor becomes the student's ally. This is demonstrated in the following case example with a sixth-grade girl who indicated she did not need or want to be seen for counseling. When asked who referred her for counseling and why, she indicated that her father and assistant principal thought she wasn't able to control her temper. She attended weekly anger management classes against her will. She claimed that she didn't need the class or help from a counselor because she was able to control her temper on her own. After a few minutes of complaining that her dad and the assistant principal were wrong in their assessment, the counselor asked her, "So, you're saying that they are wrong and you are right. What do you think if, through counseling, we could prove to them that they were wrong in sending you here and you were right all along. Would that be something that would interest you?" She responded, "You're darn right! That would be great." The counselor then asked her, "What would they tell me you were doing that would show that they were wrong about your ability to control your temper and that you were right?" She then began to describe what turned into a goal for controlling her anger.

In the second session a week later, the student said the assistant principal had been amazed when she lectured the student about breaking school rules and the student listened quietly without swearing at the assistant principal, which had been the student's typical response. The assistant principal was so impressed that she gave the student a 2-day rather than the usual 5-day suspension for her misbehavior. Similar changes occurred in the student's classes and at home as she proved to everyone that they were wrong and she was right. Three sessions was all it took to get her on track in reducing her angry outbursts significantly.

When SFBC Hasn't Worked

It is unrealistic to believe that any counseling approach will work with every student. This is true with the SFBC approach as well. Although successful with most students (I have found that 80%–85% of students reached their goals for counseling), in some instances SFBC may not be successful for various reasons. Some students may just want to complain and be heard and others are not interested in changing.

Rudy, a 15-year-old, seventh-grade male, is one of those examples. Rudy was referred to counseling because he was failing and displayed disruptive behavior in school. When asked why he thought he was sent to see me, he finally admitted that everyone in school thinks he fights too much. He claimed that he liked to fight and that "no one had ever kicked his ass," and he didn't want to quit fighting. After several unsuccessful attempts to identify exceptions to his desire to fight in order to identify a goal, the session moved in the direction of trying to identify some positive things about Rudy. Pursuing information about his grades in school, I learned that he was failing every class except science. In science he was getting a grade of B. Thinking there was now something positive on which to build, I focused on finding out how he made that instance of success possible. When asked why he did so well in science, he replied, "We get to cut stuff up." The session continued with compliments about his success in science and his academic potential if he chose to put forth effort in his other classes. When asked if he would like to continue with counseling, he declined. This case is mentioned not to disillusion readers, but to help you recognize that, even with SFBC, not every student will be successfully helped, regardless of what you try to do.

Turning Difficult Situations Into Workable Goals

Some situations presented by students may not seem appropriate for SFBC; however, reframing questions about the student's reasons for meeting with you may redirect unworkable goals into ones that can be addressed with SFBC. The following are some examples of responses that can be used to address issues that students often bring to counseling.

Students who seem only interested in knowing "Why am I this way?"

You can respond,

- "Suppose you find out why, what would you do differently then?"
  (The details of the student's answer provide the goal to pursue.)

Students claiming they are "always" sad, unhappy, depressed, and so on

- "Are you sad every moment of every day of your life?"

  (Most students answer "no." This response implies that sometimes they are not sad, which suggests exceptions.)
- "So, what is different for you then?"

Students dealing with death or loss

- "What is it about that relationship that you want to continue?" or
- "How would . . . want you to go on with your life?" or
- "What was good about your life with . . . that you want to keep going?"

  (The answers to these questions provide the goal.)

Students who make excuses for why they can't or won't make changes

- "You continue to do . . . (self-defeating behavior); therefore, you must be getting something out of it. So, what's the reason you want to change?"

  (Information in the student's response then provides the goal.)

Students who give "yes, but" reasons
for why they can't overcome their difficulties

This particular pattern of student response can leave you feeling stuck. You can apply the following technique to use the "yes, but" pattern to establish a goal or identify a solution. After a series of "yes, but" responses, agree with one of the student's "but" responses. After the student comes back with another "yes, but" response, the "but" will usually contain a goal or solution. Consider this example: A student who is failing in school because she is not completing her homework has stated that she knows that one of the solutions is to do her homework as soon as she gets home from school. You rephrase her statement by saying the following:

- "So, one thing you would like to accomplish as a result of seeing me is to do your homework as soon as you get home from school." The student "yes, buts" your statement by saying,

- "*Yes*, I want to do my homework then, *but* it's too noisy in the house so I can't do my homework." You respond,
- "I agree. I don't see how you would ever manage to get your homework done in a noisy house." The student replies,
- "*Yes, but* I guess I could do my homework at my friend Joan's house after school because it's quiet over there."

As you can see in this example, the student's last "yes, but" response revealed something the student can accomplish to help solve the problem.

ADMINISTRATORS' USE OF SOLUTION-FOCUSED PRINCIPLES WHEN STUDENTS ARE REFERRED FOR DISCIPLINE

School administrators can implement many aspects of the solution-focused approach when students are referred for disciplinary action. Traditionally, one of the administrator's duties in school is to function as a disciplinarian. They are responsible for dealing with students who are disruptive in the classroom or on the bus, who get into fights, who are absent or tardy, who fail academically, who harass others, and who are disrespectful to teachers and students. Students who involuntarily report to the administrator's office typically have negative expectations regarding their encounter with the principal or assistant principal. Administrators use various approaches ranging from threats to suspension to try to reform misguided students—often to no avail as students frequently repeat the same offenses that led them to the administrator's office in the first place. Solution-focused counseling techniques offer an alternative to the traditional confrontational methods that are so often used.

Osborn (1999) reports that confrontation actually increases client resistance in counseling. In contrast, solution-focused counseling elicits and amplifies nonproblematic actions of involuntary clients, which lead to cooperation. The solution-focused counseling model allows administrators to remain neutral in discussing the complaints that prompted the referral and in determining what the referring person thinks the student needs to change. This neutrality is an advantage because it helps students remain more open to the input of administrators. With this in mind, administrators can use the following format and prompts to implement the solution-focused approach with reluctant students. The approach presented here is an integration of my ideas and those reported in DeJong and Berg (1998).

SOLUTION-FOCUSED GOAL–FORMULATED SEQUENCE FOR RELUCTANT AND MANDATED STUDENTS

The first step is to describe to students how the meeting will be different from what typically might be expected when being sent to an administrator. Emphasizing this different approach is essential in getting students to cooperate. The following introduction is an example of how you could initiate a meeting with a referred student.

> I imagine that you're thinking being sent to me really (is a waste of your time, ticks you off, stinks, is frustrating, etc.). My guess is that in the past when you have been sent to someone because of something you may have done that got you in trouble, you were either punished or suspended. Today, I would like to try something a little different with you. I realize that this is an unpleasant experience for you to go through. Both you and I would rather that you not be here. And my guess is that you would like me to get off your back. Would you agree?
>
> I would like to help you look at ways you can avoid having to be sent to me by examining some of your past experiences that have worked to help you be successful in school. I know there have been times when that has happened, and if we can discover how you made that happen for yourself, you can avoid being in this situation again. To accomplish this, I'm going to ask you some really tough questions that will probably be hard to answer, but I think you are up to the task. How does that sound to you?

If the student responds that he or she isn't interested in the offer, indicate to the student other options that are warranted for the situation, which may include suspension or other established penalties.

1. Problem Description and Attempts at Solutions

After establishing willingness on a student's part to participate in a solution-focused approach, it is important to determine the student's view of the reason for being sent to you. As the student reveals his or her perspective on the situation, pay attention for clues about what the student may want and be willing to do. The following examples illustrate what you might say:

- "What is your understanding of why we are meeting today?" (Be prepared to share what you know about the referral.)
- "What have you thought about trying next time you have this difficulty but haven't tried yet?" "How might that be helpful?"

2. Goal Formulation

The next step helps students clarify what they need to do to avoid repeating the difficulty that resulted in being sent to you. Helping students recognize the reciprocal relationship that evolves as a result of their different behavior helps them see the big picture that yields more positive outcomes for them. Follow up by trying to obtain a commitment to try even a small step to improve the relationship between the student and the referring party and significant others in his or her life. The following are examples of what you could say to the student.

- "What does your (teacher, parent, bus driver, lunchroom attendant, etc.) think you need to do differently?"
- "If you were to decide to do that, what would be different between you and your (teacher, parent, etc.)?"
- Continue by asking, "What would be different between you and (significant others)?"
- "Is that something you could and would do?"
- "At a minimum, what would you say that you have to do differently in order to . . . ?"

After the goal is formulated, next ask the miracle question and inquire about exceptions/instances of success. These steps are similar to what has been previously presented in this book; therefore, only prompts for the solution-focused sequence will be presented in this section. The scaling and message-writing components of SFBC can be omitted to save time.

3. Miracle Question

- "Remember when I told you I was going to ask you some tough questions? Well, here is one of them."

Regarding the student:

- "Let's imagine that when you went to bed tonight a miracle happened while you were sleeping and when you woke up the next morning this problem that brought you here today was gone. What would you notice that you would be doing differently? (Get specific behavioral details.)
- "What will be the first thing that you notice?"

Regarding significant others:

- "Who would notice that this miracle had happened?"
- "When . . . notices that, what will . . . do differently?" (Get specific behavioral details.)
- "When . . . does that, what will be different for you?" or "How do you think you will react?"

What else questions:

- "What else would you notice that you would be doing differently after this miracle?" (Get specific behavioral details and follow with "regarding significant others" questions above.)

4. Past Successes/Exceptions

- "Tell me about some time when you made some or even just a little bit of this miracle happen." (Compliment the student's ability to overcome the situation.)

5. Moving Toward a Solution

- "Suppose you were to pretend that the miracle happened. What would be the first small thing you would do?"
- "How might that be helpful?" or

- "What's it going to take for part of the miracle to happen?"
- "Is that something that could happen? If so, what makes you think so?"

6. Conclusion

If the student is concrete and detailed in answering the miracle question and instances of success, compliment the student for the efforts and willingness to work with you on the issue. You may suggest one of the following to the student:

- "In the next couple of days, why don't you give the things you came up with today a try and pop in my office to let me know how it turned out."
- "Pick one day this week and pretend that the miracle has happened and observe what a difference it makes. Stop by my office to let me know how it worked out for you."
- "In our talk today, it has become clear to me that you have what it takes to make things better for yourself. How about trying some of those things this week and then come back to see me to tell me how it worked."

If the student is vague in answering the miracle question, give compliments for any positive actions, thoughts, or ideas expressed by the student and suggest, "This week, when things are a little better, notice what you have done to make it better and stop by my office to tell me about it."

SUMMARY

Students who need assistance are not always willing to accept help from counselors and administrators. This is especially true if students view the counselors or administrators as telling them what they have to do to satisfy the school. Solution-focused counseling avoids this frequent source of student resistance by framing the discussion around the student's goals and strengths, not the school's requirements.

The solution-focused methods presented in this chapter provide you with tools to redirect reluctant students into willing participants in the process of improving their success in school.

The next chapter highlights several modifications and tools that increase the efficiency and applicability of the solution focused approach. These include referral forms focusing on desired changes, modified 15- to 20-minute sessions, group applications, guided imagery, and the use of puppets with young students.

CHAPTER SEVEN

Expanding Solution-Focused Concepts

Solution-focused concepts can be useful in other school counseling situations as well, as discussed in this chapter. Kral (1994) developed an abbreviated version of this approach in which interviews are initiated with scaling. Beginning a counseling session with this part of the model shortens it from approximately 40 minutes to 15 or 20 minutes. I have found this approach effective with children as young as 6 years old who have difficulty conceptualizing miracles and with those students who have difficulty identifying a goal for counseling.

Another approach is being used to assist teachers who refer students for counseling. Dr. Lou Bryant (personal communication, September 15, 1994), a practicing school counselor in St. Louis, Missouri, has found solution-oriented referral forms to be helpful in directing teachers' attention to what's working for students despite their troubles. The referral form also helps teachers see how they contribute to students' successes. This triggers a reciprocal pattern—teachers' perceptions of students are affected, causing changes in their reactions, which in turn lead to changes in students' behavior.

Dr. Donald Nims and Letitia Holland-Cundiff have used puppets with SFBC. Using puppets, young children were able to express themselves more clearly.

Whereas the brief nature of SFBC enables counselors to see more students for counseling, adapting this method for use with groups expands efficiency even more. Use of solution-focused counseling groups in schools has been reported by LaFountain et al. (1996). Elementary school counselors also have experienced success with SFBC methods in groups, as discussed in this chapter. Solution-focused guided imagery was recently developed (Sklare, Sabella, & Petrosco, 2003) as a single-session approach that can be used in a group setting with both small and large audiences. This group technique will be presented later in this chapter.

THE 20-MINUTE SESSION

Circumstances often arise during the day when a 40-minute counseling session is just not feasible. Students' and counselors' schedules may limit the time for counseling contact, and some teachers may not be willing to allow their students to miss an entire class for counseling. Many students are only willing to see their counselors during their 20-minute lunch break at school. Short attention spans of some students may restrict follow-through with the complete model. This is particularly true of younger children in the early elementary grades. Because of their inability to concentrate for long periods of time, the shorter form of solution-focused counseling may be more appropriate.

Scaling

Faced with these obstacles, Kral (1994) found a remedy in an abbreviated application of SFBC that appears to be effective with students at all grade levels. Counselors initiate this shortened interview by asking students to rate where they are now on a scale from 0 to 100, with 100 representing their lives being perfect for them and 0 representing when things are the worst they can ever be. For elementary school students, the 0 can be defined as the saddest they could ever be and the 100 could be the happiest they could possibly be, except when receiving a gift. (Receiving gifts is excluded because it depends on circumstances outside the individual rather than reflecting actions the student might take.) Kral (1994) expanded the scale from 10 to 100 because he found that many students responded to the 10-point scale with fractional responses, such as 4½. With the expanded range, students could instead give a response like 45, which made it easier to measure smaller degrees of success. The extremes are stated to give students perspective on their current situation. By comparing their current status with a worst-case scenario, students are helped to recognize the strengths they have used to keep from hitting bottom. At the other end of the continuum, students see that by using their strengths, they can achieve beyond the best it has been so far. A "sad face" to "smiley face" continuum can also be used with younger children. Here are examples of leads that you can use to initiate this approach:

- "You're looking down in the dumps because of this situation that you have come to see me for. If we had a scale of 0–100, with 0 being the lowest you could picture yourself being and 100 being when things would be perfect for you, where do you think you are right now?"
- "You don't seem to be sure what you want to accomplish in counseling. Perhaps it would help if you were to rate yourself on a scale of 0–100, with 0 being the saddest you could ever be and 100 being the happiest you could ever be, except for getting a gift. Where would you put yourself right now?"
- "So, you have been sent to me and you're not sure why, but you do know that school isn't going as well as you would like it to go. Maybe to get us started, you may want to consider this. If you had a scale with numbers from 0 to 100, and 0 is when things here at school were at rock bottom or the worst you could imagine and 100 is when things are ideal or the best you could ever imagine them to be for you at school, where do you think you are right now?"

Determining the Highest Rating Achieved

After students select a rating, ask them to assess the highest score they have ever achieved. Two possibilities exist: (a) in the past they have had a higher score than at present or (b) their present rating is the highest it's ever been.

Higher Past Ratings

When higher ratings are reported in the past, students reveal to you and to themselves the presence of solutions that are not being applied. The same types of questions as described in Chapter 3 are implemented—questions that identify instances of success or exceptions to problems. Ask students to determine what was different between then and now and what students were doing before to bring about their higher ratings. The following interventions illustrate this:

- "From what you're saying, you are now at 56, and you have been as high as 75. What was going on with you when you were at 75? How is that different from what is going on right now?"
- "So, you think because you were being monitored closely, things were better. I bet there were times when you weren't being monitored closely that you still were doing a 75. Isn't that right?"
- "And how did you manage to keep yourself at a 75 then, even when you weren't being watched so closely?"
- "It's fantastic that you could have slacked off but, by telling yourself that, you didn't. That shows you have willpower."

When the Present Rating Is the Highest

If the present rating is the highest it has ever been, ask students what is the lowest they have ever been. The purpose is to determine how students have improved to where they are now. Exploring the differences between their actions related to their lower scores and their behaviors associated with higher ratings helps students chart how they have used their resources to achieve their highest rating and provides them with tools to advance even further. This is demonstrated in the following interventions:

- "What you're telling me is that right now you're at 43 and that is the highest you have ever been. I'm also thinking that you have been lower than 43, and I'm curious—how far down have you been prior to your working so hard to get where you are today?"
- "So, you have been at an 18 and now you're at a 43. What did you do to move yourself up to where you are now? How did you make that happen for yourself? I know that had to be real hard, knowing all that you were going through at that time."

Moving to a Higher Level

For those students who have previously had higher ratings, focus on how these students will again move to their highest level. Ask what students have to do and how they can apply their resources to their present situation to achieve success as before. For those presently at their highest rating, inquiring how their past successes can be used to improve even more helps students move up the scale. Here are examples of counselor interventions that facilitate this:

- "You are at a 56 right now, and you have been as high as a 75; I'm wondering how you can get yourself back up to that 75?"
- "What are you going to have to do to return to your highest rating?"
- "You're the highest you have ever been, and you know what you have done to get there. When you are a little bit higher, what will you be doing then that you are not doing now?"
- "Recognizing all the hard work it took to get to where you are, what's it going to take for you to gain a few more points on your scale?"

Message/Task

Kral (1994) suggests counselors assign a task to conclude the abbreviated session. Tasks are similar to those issued in the message writing discussed in Chapters 3 and 4. Homework tasks are nonspecific. They encourage students to notice what's better, to do the things that have worked, to pretend they are 10% better, and so forth. Here are some examples of tasks:

- Begin to do those things you have done in the past that have been proven to work.
- Notice what you're doing that tells you that you are doing better.
- Pretend you've improved 10% by doing those things that will make this happen for you.

I find that writing a very brief message and giving it to students is a more effective way to reinforce students for taking actions. With the brevity of the interview, fewer notes are taken and less is said; therefore, the message is shorter, like the interview. The message is constructed using the same format described in Chapters 3 and 4.

A CASE OF ABBREVIATED SOLUTION-FOCUSED COUNSELING

The following case with Lincoln, an 8-year-old third-grader, illustrates the abbreviated version of the solution-focused approach. Lincoln's mother referred him to me for counseling in an attempt to help him before sending him to a psychiatrist for medication because of his misbehavior, angry outbursts, and failing in school.

As the meeting began, Lincoln was asked to identify where he was on the 100-point scale. After briefly discussing his rating, he indicated his lowest score was a 0, just a few months ago when his dad had died (he began to cry while recalling this). After I made several empathetic comments, he was asked where he was on the scale now. Lincoln responded he was at 10. When queried how he got from a 0 to a 10, after some thought he responded, "I remember things like going camping and Disney World with my dad and the good times we had." He also recalled the one time he had briefly talked with his mother about how he missed his dad (he hadn't discussed his dad's death with anyone else).

As he continued, I asked him to identify where he was at that moment on the scale. He replied he was at 20. When queried how he was able to move up 10 points in just 5 minutes, he responded, "Talking about my dad when I think about missing him." To help Lincoln apply the resources he had just discovered, I asked Lincoln what he would be doing when he would be at a 30. He replied, "I could talk to my mom about my dad after dinner when I need to."

The following brief message was given to Lincoln:

I am really impressed with how aware you are of your feelings about your dad. You know it's okay to feel sad that he died, but you also know that it is important to talk about him with your mother when you become sad. Remembering the good times you had with him when you went to Disney World and camping helps pick you up.

To keep you on target to moving to a 30, notice what you are doing this week to make things better for yourself.

For his second session, Lincoln appeared in my office with a smile on his face. When asked the reason he was so happy, he responded that he was seeing me and getting out of class. When I asked, "What's better this week?" he reported he was at 100 on his scale. He stated he had been having regular conversations with his mother about his dad. He indicated his mother was also happier as a result of his talking to her about his father. Lincoln also reported that he had earned free-play time at school every day during the past week. When asked if that was different, he replied, "It sure is, because this was the first time all year that I earned play time." When queried about how this was different and how he made that happen, he responded that he raised his hand before answering the teacher's questions and he stayed in his seat until the teacher gave him permission to get up. He also listened and did what his teacher asked him to do.

In the third and last session, 2 weeks after the second session, Lincoln reported continued improvement. His conversations with his mother about his dad continued but with less frequency because he felt less sad. Lincoln also was improving his grades in school. In addition to his previous changes, he began to walk in straight lines in the hall as the teacher requested, remained in his seat on the school bus, and started hanging around students who were less rowdy. This led to fewer episodes of trouble and more free-play time. His mother was so impressed with Lincoln's progress that she did not consult a psychiatrist and she referred Lincoln's younger brother for counseling as well.

30-Second Counseling

I have found that students have an uncanny ability to remember their scaled ratings and what these numbers represent behaviorally. Therefore, counselors and administrators can offer quick, 30-second pep sessions while passing students in the hall, at the bus, or in the lunchroom by inquiring verbally or nonverbally where students are on their scales at the moment. Thumbs up or hand gestures reflecting okay from you also can show students that they are being acknowledged for their efforts. Nonverbal expressions that support students to move higher on their scales also can be given by pointing to students and then up toward the ceiling. This private conversation illustrates a bond with students in which only they know what is being communicated. If a significant drop in a rating is noted, this signals that an appointment may be needed to get the student back on track.

COUNSELING REFERRAL FORM

Another helpful tool is a solution-based counseling form developed by Lou Bryant (personal communication, September 15, 1994) to be used by teachers and administrators to refer students to counseling (see Table 7.1). The form helps those who are initiating referrals to identify specific behaviors to be addressed and to notice when some parts of desired behaviors already have occurred. This section also implies that the person making the referral may be doing something to make things better, and it alerts the person to notice what that may be. The third and final question on the form enables referring parties to rate students' present behaviors and note past successes. The tenor of the form is to provide counselors information about possible goals for students. However, an even greater benefit stems from helping referring parties notice successes and what is working for students and for themselves.

USE OF PUPPETS IN SOLUTION-FOCUSED BRIEF COUNSELING

In another application of SFBC, Dr. Donald Nims and Letitia Holland-Cundiff used puppets to facilitate the counseling process when working with young children (personal communication, April 7, 2004). Many young children find it difficult to discuss their problems but find it easier to act out what they cannot talk out. Puppets help those students express what they can't express in words. This is especially helpful in the first step of goal setting in the SFBC process.

Collaboration with parents and teachers is a key element when using puppets in SFBC. Inappropriate behaviors that lead to counseling are often the result of underlying issues that stem from

Table 7.1   Solution-Focused Brief Counseling Referral Form

Student's Name _____ Grade _____

Date _____

Counselor _____

Person Referring _____

1. What, in your opinion, will this student be doing differently (goal) when there is resolution of the problem(s) for which he or she was referred?

    What would be evidence of a solid first step toward meeting this goal?

2. Indicate times when parts of the goal have already been achieved.

    How would you account for the student's progress toward the goal at those times?

3. On a scale of 0–10 (0 lowest to 10 highest),
    a. Where would you rate the present behavior of this student?

    b. What is the highest rating this student has reached, in your observation?

    c. Rate your level of optimism about the possibility of change for this student.

divorce, loss, or abuse. Prior awareness of these issues enables the counselor to be an active participant in the puppet play.

The following case demonstrates the use of puppets in SFBC with young children. Emily, an 8-year-old, was referred by her teacher to the school counselor because she was withdrawn in class. Her mother reported that she was increasingly uncooperative and aggressive at home. The counselor was aware that Emily's parents were divorced and that recently her mother had remarried and they now live with her new stepfather. Emily was given a hand puppet made of two pieces of neutral-colored material stitched together (Blackwell, 1997). She was asked to use markers to draw a face on her puppet that represented how she was feeling at that time. She drew a sad face. Emily, talking to the counselor through her puppet, indicated she was sad because she and her mother had moved in with her stepdad in a different home. The counselor asked Emily's puppet what she would be doing if she weren't sad anymore. Emily described doing fun things with her mother like going to the park as they used to do before her mother remarried.

In the second step of the SFBC sequence, the counselor used a hand puppet that looked like a wizard with magical powers to ask the miracle question. As the wizard puppet asked the miracle question, he waved a magic wand and told Emily's puppet that when Emily wakes up she is at home with her mom and stepdad and she is happy. The wizard puppet asked her what she would be doing differently that showed she was happy. Emily said she would wake up and be thinking about the fun things she was going to do that day like going to the park, the mall, or playing with her friends. When asked the reciprocal relationship question about what her mother would notice that would be different, Emily said she would smile at her mother when she came in to wake her up. When asked how her mother would respond to this, Emily answered that her mother would smile back, give her a hug, and they would go down together to the kitchen for breakfast. The counselor's puppet then asked Emily what her stepfather would notice that showed a miracle had happened. She said he would see her smiling and laughing and he would join in, too. Together the three of them would eat breakfast and make their plans for the day. Emily would then get dressed and make her bed without being asked. She would even clean her room. She smiled and said her mother would really be surprised at that. Then they would all go to the park.

In the third step, the counselor used the puppet to provide Emily with the opportunity to identify exceptions or instances of success in having some of her miracle occur even a little. Emily described how happy she was when her mother and stepfather took her one time to the park before they got married. She remembered that afterward, when her mother asked her to help with the laundry, she did so willingly and even cleaned up her own room. The counselor made a point to compliment her and asked how she knew to clean her room even though she wasn't asked. She said it made her happy when her mother was happy. The counselor affirmed her response. At this point the counselor selected puppets to portray Emily's mother and stepfather. Together with Emily's puppet, they role-played some of the miracle as Emily described it, waking up, greeting her mother, having breakfast together, making her bed, cleaning her room, and going to the park.

Scaling is the next step in the SFBC process. This includes using a laminated strip of cardboard that has ten faces on a continuum, from an angry-looking face to a happy-looking face. Emily's puppet was asked to take a marker and circle the face that represented where she was on the scale related to achieving her miracle. Emily circled the number 7 face. Emily's puppet was asked to explain the reason for her rating. Emily, speaking for her puppet, replied that she cleaned her room without being asked. When the counselor's puppet then asked what would she be doing when she was at an 8, Emily's puppet described that she would be doing her homework with her mother and then her stepfather would read her favorite story with her before she went to bed.

Consistent with SFBC, a message consisting of compliments, the bridge, and the task is written and given to the child at the end of the session. In this case, Emily was praised and encouraged for talking about her feelings about her mother and stepfather and for her willingness to role-play her miracle with the puppets. The counselor complimented Emily for her success in achieving some of her miracle as indicated by the exceptions to when she has the problem. This was particularly the case in how she cleaned her room without being asked and how important it was to Emily that her mother be happy, too. Emily's task was to pay attention to her feelings when they are more positive and notice what she is doing to make that happen. She was also asked to notice the things she does at home and at school that help her move up one number on her scale of happy faces. The counselor continued to collaborate with Emily's teacher and mother to follow her progress. In subsequent sessions, Emily was given the opportunity to draw a new face on the other side of her puppet. These sessions began with scaling to determine where Emily was at that moment and followed the second and subsequent sessions previously described in this book. Emily showed significant progress both at home and at school. She was able to express her feelings regarding her new family makeup. She was more animated in her schoolwork, and the relationship with her mother improved.

The following two cases also show how puppets can be used effectively with SFBC with young children. Lisa, 8 years old, was dealing with the effects of stress and some depression. She was exposed to severe domestic violence. She was having nightmares and difficulty sleeping. Her goal was to sleep at night with happy dreams. Puppets were used to help show her how to express her feelings and thoughts in a way that was not scary. In addition, puppets helped Lisa visualize her miracle of sleeping peacefully. Follow-up sessions indicated a steady scaling increase toward reaching her goal. Her mother reported that Lisa had no more nightmares.

Jason, 4 years old, was also dealing with stress and with severe behavior problems in preschool. He had experienced abuse and had had three foster care placements. Jason was referred to the counselor for fighting with his peers. His goal was to play without fighting. Following the miracle question, Jason and the counselor used puppets to act out his miracle of interacting with others in more appropriate ways while playing basketball or board games, even when he missed a shot or lost a turn. He would be able to walk away without fighting. Scaling indicated movement from a 5 to a 6 on the continuum of faces. His behaviors improved in his current foster care placement and he was able to get along better with his peers.

SFBC is very relevant for working with young children. Puppets are a valuable aid in facilitating this process of helping children find acceptable solutions to the many issues they face.

SOLUTION-FOCUSED GROUP AND CLASSROOM COUNSELING

Solution-focused concepts can be applied to group settings as well. The group application resembles family counseling in that students provide feedback to each other based on their observed interactions in class.

Group Counseling

The following description shows an elementary counselor's (Margaret Cavitt, personal communication, February 15, 1996) adaptation of SFBC to a small-group setting. The group was established in response to a first-grade teacher's difficulty with a group of five boys with behavior problems. The group was scheduled to meet for 30 minutes once a week for 6 weeks. Note that a mirror is needed for each of the meetings.

First Meeting

Students are asked why they thought they were asked to participate in the group. Group members identify their behaviors in and out of class that are a problem for them and for their teacher. After making a commitment to learn how to improve their behaviors, students are asked to identify what their behaviors would look like if by magic their problem had disappeared. Furthermore, students are asked who would notice and what they would see as being different in the students once the problem had disappeared. Each member responds to this question while others in the group are encouraged to contribute what they would see them do differently as well.

After all members have had the opportunity to respond, they are asked to rate themselves on a scale, indicating where they are from 0 to 10. A 0 represents never doing any of the behaviors just described, and 10 indicates the described behaviors are happening all the time. Students also are asked the reasons they rated themselves as they did. Following their self-ratings, students are asked to make a promise to themselves, in front of a mirror and the group, about the things they would do to move up one number on the scale. The counselor records each student's promises on an index card that is photocopied and then given to the student. The group is then dismissed.

Second Meeting and the Four Subsequent Meetings

Students are surveyed concerning improvements since their last meeting. Group members are encouraged to describe things they have noticed that were better about the behavior of each of the other members during the week. Then they are asked to rate themselves on the 0–10 scale. This is followed by cheerleading and detailing how members made the changes. Students reflect on the effects their improved behaviors had on others and on themselves. If reported ratings regress, students are supported for their efforts to prevent their scores from going even lower, and they are asked what they would do differently next time to move higher on their scales.

Members discuss new promises they would like to make to themselves that would raise their ratings one more place on the scale. Students return to the mirror to make promises to themselves, and the counselor records, copies, and distributes the revised promises to the children.

Before the meeting concludes, members are asked to share with each other the improvements they have seen and expect to continue to see in one another. The group is then dismissed. Sessions three through six follow the same format.

Result

The teacher who referred the students for counseling reported positive results in the students' behavior. The five students improved so much that they had each been recognized as student of the week in their class at least once during the term. Because of the counselor's success with this and other solution-based groups, the school principal has requested she spend more of her time doing counseling.

Classroom Counseling

A solution-focused classroom counseling program was implemented by Jed Turner (personal communication, April 2, 1995), a counselor from Liberty Elementary School in Oldham County, Kentucky. He sought to assist teachers with fourth-grade and fifth-grade students who were not getting along with each other, failing to become a cohesive unit, and not taking responsibility for their behaviors. The classes had become disruptive, and learning was being compromised. Several teachers specifically asked for his help, saying they were at their wit's end and didn't know what to do.

In response to this request, Turner developed a five-session classroom counseling plan adapted from the SFBC approach he had been using with individual students. The first two meetings, of about an hour to an hour and a half each, are conducted on 2 successive days. The third meeting, of about 60 minutes, is conducted 2 or 3 days after the second meeting, and the final two meetings, of 30–45 minutes each, are held 1 and 2 weeks later. The following describes the strategies Turner used with one class to implement solution-focused classroom counseling.

First Meeting

The first session opened with an explanation of why the counselor was there and an overview of the five meetings in which they would work together to solve the problems of the class. Ground rules were established for participation (as examples, everyone would have the right to speak, there would be no judging of what others say, students or the teacher would not be identified by name when describing situations but instead would be referred to in general terms such as "a kid in here," "some students in this class," or "the teacher"). Comments were recorded on newsprint and saved for later use. The teacher participated in the process along with the students.

The meeting began with students describing their perceptions of the problems in their class. Before the first meeting, the counselor alerted the teacher that she might hear comments that might not be complimentary and solicited her willingness to participate. Before starting the session, the counselor reminded students of their teacher's commitment to making things better by inviting the counselor to help them resolve their difficulties. The counselor emphasized the teacher's willingness to hear students' views of her even if they were not positive.

The counselor initiated the session by asking, "What is the problem in this class?" All comments were recorded on newsprint. Every student was encouraged to participate. After all the responses were recorded, the counselor explained that there were always positives along with negatives in all situations, and therefore they were to think about the positive things in class, so they could discuss them when the counselor returned the following day. This assignment concluded the session.

Second Meeting (the Next Day)

The meeting began with students and the teacher identifying the positive things observed in the class. In this case, students' responses included that the teacher was fair, the teacher did listen and try to help, and some people didn't criticize or make fun of others (negative goals were not reframed into positive goals at this time). During this sequence, students were asked to identify when they observed the positive things occurring.

Next, the counselor asked a version of the miracle question to elicit what the classroom would look like if all their problems were gone. "Let's pretend that this chalk (pointer, ruler) has magical powers, and when I wave it over the classroom, a miracle will take place and everything will be as you want it to be in here." (The generic miracle question could also be used.) As students responded to the miracle question, negative goals were reframed into positive goals. As discussed in Chapters 2 and 3, the specific details that described a picture of each goal were clarified and listed on newsprint.

Students usually claimed the miracle was impossible to achieve. The counselor agreed that it's impossible to have 100% of everything and be perfect; however, the goal was to work toward getting some of their miracle to happen. This was followed by the question, "Is everybody in the class willing to make that commitment?"

A form of scaling was used at this point. Students held up fingers on their raised hands to indicate the extent of their commitment to improve. No fingers represented no commitment at all; five fingers meant they would be willing to do almost anything to make the miracle happen. Barriers to students being more committed were explored with questions such as, "What's keeping you from being committed?" or "When you are committed—just one finger more—what will you be doing then?"

The second meeting concluded with a homework task. The students and teacher were to write what they were going to do to make their miracle happen. The counselor emphasized the importance of students' focusing on what they would do and not what others were doing or not doing. It was important that students remained focused on what they would do and took responsibility for their behaviors. (Unless this is emphasized, students tend to focus on others' behaviors.) Referring to the posted chart listing the positive things that were identified at the start of the second meeting (exceptions) reminded students that some of these things were already happening. The homework assignment was to be completed before the counselor returned to the class several days later.

Third Meeting (2 or 3 Days Later)

Students read their homework assignments aloud. Then the counselor asked the class to identify when some of these instances of success had occurred during the past several days. As these occasions were noted, the counselor cheerled and helped students detail how they made these events happen.

A line with numbers ranging from 0 to 10 was drawn on the board, with 0 representing when the class was at its worst and 10 being the miracle day. Students were asked to rate where they thought the class was right now and what they had done to move up to that rating from a 0. (If students' ratings vary, their scores can be averaged to determine a group rating.) Students were then asked what they would have to do to move up the scale a point and how they would make this happen. Students were asked, "What differences would the teacher notice that would tell her that things had improved 10%?" The teacher also gave input during the entire sequence.

Next, the counselor gave a task. Students and their teacher were (a) to notice between now and the next meeting the things that they and others in class were doing to move up one number on the scale and (b) to compliment each other when they observed those positive things happening. This activity was designed to initiate a change from a class climate that was negative and critical to positive and complimentary.

Fourth Meeting (1 Week Later)

The session started by surveying where students perceived the class to be on their scale and what had happened during the week that had led them to this rating. The counselor cheerled and complimented students' efforts and elicited the details of how students managed to cause these changes to happen for themselves. They were again asked to identify what they would need to do to advance another 10% on their scale. The session, which lasted about 30–40 minutes, concluded in the same manner as the third meeting, with an assignment to notice and compliment one another when things were getting better so these successes could be discussed during the final meeting.

Fifth Meeting (2 Weeks Later)

The format for this session was the same as for the previous meeting. At the end of this meeting, the counselor assigned the class to continue to do those things that were working and would move the class on a path to reach a 10.

Results

The class continued to improve without further counselor intervention. The teacher was extremely pleased with the results of the classroom counseling sessions. Not only were things better for her and for the students, but she also had learned from students' feedback how to be a more effective teacher. Probably most important, the teacher was now thinking solutions instead of problems and was looking for successes to highlight rather than failures. This was both empowering and a boost to her students' self-esteem.

After hearing about the success of this solution-focused classroom counseling, several other teachers requested this experience for their classes. They enjoyed similar results.

SOLUTION-FOCUSED GUIDED IMAGERY

Solution-focused guided imagery is the blending of SFBC with guided imagery techniques to expand the practice of SFBC to group settings. The solution-focused guided imagery method presented here was developed by me and was previously published (Sklare, Sabella, & Petrosco, 2003). Although the participants who originally participated in solution-focused guided imagery were adults, it appears that this approach would be effective in a secondary school setting as well. Due to the lack of personal communication between the counselor and individual participants and the writing skills needed to complete this activity, young children (elementary school age) may not be able to comprehend or complete what is being asked of them with this procedure. Therefore, this approach is recommended for use with clients who are adolescents or older.

Solution-focused guided imagery uses guided imagery techniques to lead group participants through a solution-focused "journey." Using a series of solution-focused interventions similar to those described earlier in this book, counselors guide participants in each step to close their eyes and vividly imagine themselves thinking, feeling, and behaving in ways that would demonstrate that they are resolving their problems. After reading each of the 15 steps aloud, counselors ask participants to write what they had imagined in a booklet consisting of 15 pages with one step per page. The activity takes approximately 40–45 minutes to complete. The size of the group is not limited. This method has been found effective with very small groups as well as larger ones (Sklare, Sabella, & Petrosco, 2003). Appendix B contains detailed, step-by-step directions for the process.

The activity can be more structured in the first step when students with similar difficulties are in the same group. Examples might include students who are repeatedly tardy or absent, students who tend to have a pattern of getting into fights, students who have trouble getting along with others, students who are struggling to get better grades, or students who are trying to decide what to do after graduation. With a group of students with similar issues, the common problem would be mentioned in Step 1. As an example, the facilitator might say, "Think about your recurring problem of being tardy to class that you would like to overcome. Rate the severity of this problem for you from 0 (the worst it has ever been) to 10 (nonexistent)."

SUMMARY

Even when counseling sessions are limited to 30 minutes or less, an abbreviated form of SFBC has yielded positive results. Effectiveness has been enhanced by using a referral form that helps the referring party identify the specific changes students will make and have already made to improve their situations. Solution-focused principles have been applied to group and classroom counseling situations and to the use of puppets in counseling. Last, the blending of solution-focused and guided imagery procedures can serve to expand this approach for use with unlimited numbers of students at the same time, enabling school counselors to serve even more students efficiently and effectively.

FINAL THOUGHTS

In closing, it seems appropriate to highlight the unique advantages of SFBC. Although it is not the answer for every client, the approach is remarkably versatile—it can work for any number of problems or diagnoses. Its versatility stems from the simple fact that the goal in counseling is the client's goal, not the counselor's, parent's, teacher's, or principal's goal. So long as clients can be helped to identify what they want to achieve, regardless of the nature of the difficulty, the solution-focused approach can work.

The solution-focused approach has the added advantage of being quick. Because the effects can be observed soon after counseling begins, clients experience a heightened sense of motivation to follow through with behavioral change. The spin-offs of improved relationships with family, teachers, and friends add to the student's motivation to make positive choices.

This approach is also unique in recognizing the power of focus. It acknowledges that when counseling focuses on problems—describing them, their frequency, and their impact—clients typically tend to continue having those problems. And when counseling focuses on solutions—what works, how it works, and when—clients tend to experience more solutions to their difficulties. The bottom line: You get more of whatever you focus on. This simple tenet of SFBC is perhaps its most powerful.

I hope this book has inspired you to want to try this approach with your students. I encourage you to make the effort. You will most likely experience bumps along the road to being an effective solution-focused brief counselor. Reviewing sections of the book that address your "stuck points" or attending workshops on this approach will help fine-tune your efforts.[1]

Over the past 10 years, I have seen the effectiveness of this approach with children and youth in school settings. The exciting challenge ahead is to share the solution-focused approach with the counseling community so that more counselors, administrators, and students alike will share in the inspiring successes that will result from keeping focused on solutions.

Note

1. If you are interested in a workshop on SFBC for your school, school district, professional organization, university, or mental health

facility, you can contact me by e-mail at sklare@insightbb.com or call me at Sklare & Associates, (502) 339-5900.

One of my actual SFBC sessions is available on a training video, which follows the counseling model described in this book. The video demonstrates an initial SFBC session and follow-up session of a real case with a 10-year-old boy. The video, titled *Solution-Focused Brief Counseling: Two Actual Interviews With a Child,* is available from Microtraining Associates, who can be reached at the following e-mail: info@emicrotraining.com, Web site: www.emicrotraining. com, or phone/fax: (888) 505-5576.

Additional information about SFBC workshops and other related resources is available at http://www.sklareandassociates.com.

Appendix A

*Counseling Session
With Kasey: A Practice Exercise*

The transcript that follows* is organized to provide you with an opportunity to practice SFBC interventions. To begin, cover the page with a piece of paper or cardboard and uncover the text as you read. When you get to each ***intervention prompt*** (printed in bold-italic type within parentheses), keep the text below the prompt covered while you write out the response or intervention you would use with this client at that point in the session. Then compare your response with the one I used in the session. Because there are so many ways to respond to clients using SFBC, my responses are given only as a guide. Before you begin this exercise, you may want to look at the list of intervention prompts provided below to see if you want to review an earlier section of the book to refresh your memory about any of the SFBC steps or techniques listed.

INTERVENTION PROMPTS

(Identifying the goal)

(Clarifying the goal)

(Reframing from the absence of something to the presence of something)

---

* From *Brief Therapy With Individuals and Couples*, J. Carlson and L. Sperry (Eds.), copyright 2000 by Zeig, Tucker & Theisen, Publishers. Reprinted with permission.

(Detailing specific behaviors)

(Cheerleading)

(Hypothetical miracle question)

(Review of miracle responses)

(Question that exposes reciprocal effects)

(Summary statement)

(What else question)

(Instances of success/exceptions question)

(Keep focus on successes)

(Cheerleading and detailing specific behaviors)

(Accepting ownership statement)

(Mindmapping)

(Reinforcing mindmapping)

(Scaling)

(Assessing scale rating)

(Increased scale rating question)

(Flagging the minefield)

(Concluding the session statement)

The case that follows is the transcript of the first session with a 10-year-old African American boy who resides in the projects of a midsized city. The boy, who will be called Kasey, is in a class for students with behavior disorders. Kasey's teacher referred him to me for counseling. The strategies used in the meeting follow the model discussed in this book and are typical of most solution-focused sessions.

THE FIRST SESSION

The meeting begins with some introductory comments to help the client become more comfortable with counseling, a description of the procedures to be followed, and an explanation of informed consent. The session begins with determining the student's goal for counseling (*C* = Counselor; *K* = Kasey).

(Identifying the goal)

C: What's the reason that you are here?

K: I have problems.

C: What do you mean, you have problems?

K: I like messing with people and I like fighting.

C: Is that something that you want to stop doing?

K: Sometimes I want to stop. Sometimes I get messed with and I start to get mean.

(Reframing from the absence of something to the presence of something)

C: So if you were to stop messing sometimes, what would you be doing instead?

K: I'd watch TV, play Nintendo, and do my homework.

C: So those are the things you would do instead of messing and fighting and stuff like that?

K: Or if I were in school, I'd do my work and play.

(Clarifying the goal)

C: I think I have a picture of what you want to do. You're saying that there are times when you don't want to fight, you don't want to mess. And in those times you want to play instead, in a friendly way.

K: Yeah.

(Hypothetical miracle question)

C: Here is the first crazy question: Suppose tonight when you go to sleep, a miracle happens. Because you were sleeping you didn't know this miracle happened, and when you woke up in the morning the problem that brought you here was gone. No longer were you fighting or messing with people at all. What would be some of the things you would notice the next day that would tell you that there has been a miracle?

K: I won't be doing anything mean to them, to hurt them.

(Reframing from the absence of something to the presence of something)

C: So instead of doing mean things, what would you be doing?

K: Going over to my friends' houses to see what they are doing.

(Detailing specific behaviors)

C: So you'd go over to your friends' houses to see what they are doing, and not being mean. What would they notice that you were doing that would say to them, "Hey, Kasey . . ."

K: You've changed.

(Detailing specific behaviors)

C: What would they say that you've changed to? What would they see you doing?

K: I wouldn't be pushing them around like I used to sometimes.

(Reframing from the absence of something to the presence of something)

C: So instead of pushing them around, what would you be doing?

K: I'd just be talking to them nicely.

(Question that exposes reciprocal effects)

C: When they saw you talking to them nicely instead of pushing them around, how would they react to you? What would they do? How would they respond to you?

K: Nice.

(Detailing specific behaviors)

C: What would they be doing that would be different that would show they were being nice to you?

K: Like, when they throw the ball and I miss it, they would give me a look and say, "That's OK, try to catch it next time."

(Question that exposes reciprocal effects)

C: When this happens, how would you be different?

K: Try to help them get the ball.

(Summary statement)

C: I guess that whole thing would happen different, if you started to make that little change, and that would cause them to change, and then that would cause you to change.

K: Yeah.

(What else question)

C: Tell me, what else would be different if this miracle happened?

K: I wouldn't be calling them names. We'd be joking around but we wouldn't be calling names.

(Reframing from the absence of something to the presence of something)

C: Instead of calling names, what would you be doing?

K: I would call them by their real names instead of saying, "What's up, punk?"

(Question that exposes reciprocal effects)

C: When they heard that, what would they do?

K: *(Motions jaw dropping.)*

C: *(Laughing.)* Their jaw would drop. They would say, this is a new Kasey. They would be amazed.

K: They would.

C: You'd just blow their socks off if you did something like that? And after you did that, what would they say to you? How would they act when you talk to them that way?

K: You've changed! Sometimes they'd say, "You've changed a lot!"

(Question that exposes reciprocal effects)

C: They'd say that. How would they behave toward you?

K: They'd be nice to me.

(Detailing specific behaviors)

C: How would they act nice to you? What would tell you they were being nice to you?

K: Like I said, if I miss a ball or something, they would pat me on my back and say, "Try harder next time." Like when we play kickball and I roll it wrong, and somebody still kicks it far and straight up to me so I can catch it and I miss it, they just pat me on my back.

C: Instead of using different kinds of language and stuff, you'd call them by their names. Who would you be calling by their names?

K: Dominique, Darrell.

C: So you'd be saying, "What's up, Darrell?"

K: Yeah. That's one thing I won't change . . . saying, "What's up."

(Question that exposes reciprocal effects)

C: So if all of a sudden you started calling them by their names, saying, "What's up, Dominique?" and they are patting you on your back, what would you be doing in return?

K: Patting them back on their back, or hitting them on their shoulder.

(Summary statement and what else question)

C: In other words, you would have a different kind of relationship with them? What else would happen with this miracle?

K: I'd be different; everything would be different.

(Detailing specific behaviors)

C: What would you notice that would be different?

K: I'd get up and say, "Hello, Mom!" or "Hey y'all, wake up, everybody!"

C: So in other words, the way that you know this miracle happened is that you'd be saying, "Hello, Mom! Hello, everybody!" and you'd be up. Who would notice that this change was happening to you?

K: My whole family.

(Question that exposes reciprocal effects)

C: They would all notice? What would they say?

K: "Dang, you've changed!"

C: How would they know that Kasey had changed?

K: I'd be helping my mom cook. I'd start cooking before she gets home. Sometimes I would take care of everything. Or I do half of it and when she gets home she takes a little break and then she does the other half. Like, tacos—I do the hamburger and the lettuce, and heat up the taco shells.

C: Before she gets home? Boy, I bet she would appreciate that, wouldn't she? Helping out like that.

K: Yeah. She appreciates that. I did that yesterday. We had tacos. I heated up the taco shells and cut up some lettuce and tomatoes. She made the hamburger and everything else.

C: Wow, you've already done some of this stuff.

K: Yeah.

C: So your mom would notice that you are helping out. Who else in your family would notice this miracle?

K: My brother and sisters that I would be playing with them more often sometimes. And I would treat them nice, just like my friends.

(Detailing specific behaviors)

C: What would they see you doing that would tell them, "Hey, he's treating me different, like he treats his friends?"

K: Helping them with their homework. Usually when they ask me, I say no. Sometimes I help them, sometimes I don't. That's when I feel like being nice and I be nice.

(Question that exposes reciprocal effects)

C: So you'd help them with their homework. That would sure tell them. When they see you doing that, how would they be with you?

K: They stop treating me mean 'cause they know I'm being nice. I'm usually mean to them first.

C: So instead of being mean, they are nice to you.

K: Yeah, 'cause if I'm mean to them, they are mean to me.

C: So whatever you do to them, you get that back?

K: Yeah. Like sometimes I need help with my homework. They'd be helping me do my homework.

(Instances of success/exceptions question)

C: Let me ask you another question. Tell me about some times when some of this miracle is already happening.

K: Miracle hasn't really happened.

(Review of miracle responses)

C: Let me run some of this down for you to help remind you.

K: Okay.

C: You talked about talking instead of pushing your friends around. You talked about calling them by their name instead of putting them down and calling them by their real names. And you told me about helping your mom with the cooking yesterday. That's already happened—when you helped with the tacos.

K: Yeah.

C: How did you decide to do that?

K: I just tried to be nice for a change. I just did it.

C: Yeah, but I think there are times when you decide not to do that, but yesterday you decided to do it. How did you decide that? How did that happen for you?

K: Most of the times when I do it, I'm bored. There's nothing good on TV or I want to eat 'cause I'm hungry. Or I just want to be nice.

C: You know, my guess is that you wanted to be nice. So you have that in you.

K: Yeah.

(Cheerleading)

C: Being nice is inside your soul. And you just decide sometimes that you want to be that way.

K: Yeah. It's where I live at, it gets me all confused and I just want to be mean.

C: My guess is that you can be nice if you want to even during those times when you're confused.

K: Yeah.

(Mindmapping)

C: You have that kind of control. How do you do that? How do you make yourself be nice?

K: I just say in my head about 50 times, "Be nice, be nice, be nice."

C: Oh, so you tell yourself, "Be nice." Just like that? That works for you?

K: Yeah. 50 times. Say it 50 times and I'm nice. Sometimes it takes me only 25 times to be nice.

C: How did you figure that out?

K: I don't know. I just started saying it one day and it helped me.

(Cheerleading)

C: Yeah, that's pretty miraculous. Think about that. You were able to figure that out?

K: I figured that out myself.

C: Just by yourself! You weren't watching Oprah on TV?

K: No. Just myself.

C: You figured that out on your own. You must be really smart.

K: I remember when I started saying it. It was, I think, last year and it just happened. I was bored and didn't have nothing to do. No cartoons or nothing on and I just started saying, "Be nice, be nice. Don't go in the kitchen and burn up something. Just be nice."

C: Fantastic! So you have a tool. You can make yourself be nice by just saying that. By reminding yourself, "Be nice, be nice."

K: Yeah, 25 or 50 times.

(Instances of success/exceptions question)

C: That's amazing! Tell me about some other times when you have been able to have this miracle happen for yourself.

K: I've said, "Don't do nothing wrong 'cause you know you might get a treat." And I like treats. I like going out to eat. I just say that so many times, too.

C: So you say, "Don't be mean, be nice."

K: Yeah, don't be mean, be nice.

C: And that works, too, 'cause then you get treats.

K: Yeah. Most of the time I just say, "Be nice, don't hurt nobody."

(Cheerleading)

C: Be nice, don't hurt nobody. Wow, I'm impressed. So that works for you when you are able to do that. Does that help you to say hello, to call your friends by their names, and stop yourself pushing them? Does that work there, too?

K: Yeah, sometimes I get nice to this one guy in my class who gets real mean.

(Question that exposes reciprocal effects)

C: So if you are nice to him, what happens?

K: He's nice to me.

C: So you can start it off?

K: Yeah.

(Scaling)

C: Another question for you: If we had a scale from 0–10, with 0 being that this miracle never happens. You are fighting and messing with people all the time, all the time. You have no control over it, is a 0. With 10, you are able to be nice all the time. Where do you think you are?

K: I think I'm a 5.

(Assessing scale rating)

C: That's impressive. How have you gotten yourself to 5?

K: I used to be mean all the time until just this last year I started saying those words in my head.

C: So you say, "Be nice, don't hurt anybody."

K: Yeah. And sometimes I lose control. Sometimes I don't.

(Mindmapping)

C: Sometimes you lose control. Tell me about some times when you were going to lose control and you didn't.

K: One time I wanted to do something and my mom said no and I was about to sneak, but I didn't.

C: Wait a minute, you didn't sneak!

K: Yeah. I went outside and I was about to go through the alley and through the back door and I just turned around and took off my jacket and went back in the house.

C: You didn't sneak?

K: Yeah, I was ready to but I didn't.

C: So normally, you would have sneaked out of the house?

K: Yeah. 'Cause when she has to go to the store and she says she'll be gone 2 hours, I will sneak. It takes me like 5 minutes to get up to the pay phone and I make calls. Then it takes me about 30 minutes to get back home and I've wasted my time.

(Mindmapping)

C: How did you do it that time? How did you decide not to sneak?

K: Just turned around, took off my jacket, went back in the house and calmed down.

C: I know that's what you did, but you had to make a decision about that to be able to do that, didn't you?

K: Oh, yeah. I just thought I'd get in trouble 'cause sometimes she says she'll be back in 2 hours but that's when she wants me to sneak. She'll tell me a story 'cause she doesn't want me to go anywhere. She gets back home early and she says, "Where's Kasey? He's not supposed to go outside when I'm gone!"

C: Oh, I see. So in other words, you decided you didn't want to get in trouble? That's different for you, isn't it?

K: Yeah. I only did it five times.

C: Oh. That's a lot! A lot. 'Cause you didn't want to get in trouble.

K: Right.

(Cheerleading)

C: You know, Kasey, that says something to me about you. That says that you respect your mom and yourself.

K: Yeah. Sometimes I have sneaked out when she told me not to.

(Keep focus on successes)

C: But those five times were different, for you were able to decide that you were going to listen, and going to show respect, that you were going to show that you care enough about yourself to not get yourself in trouble. That says you can do it when you want to. How did you do that, make it happen this time?

K: I don't know. For some reason, I just did. Like a miracle. Usually when I sneak out when she tells me not to and then comes back early because she forgot her card or something. When I get back home and she's home . . . yipes! I'm in trouble.

(Accepting ownership statement)

C: Yeah, but you've thought that before, haven't you? And you still went out, didn't you?

K: Yeah.

C: So it had to be different.

K: I just got tired of getting in trouble.

C: So when you think it through . . .

K: Yeah, when I think it long enough before she leaves. I'll be sitting on the front porch thinking before she goes, "Do I want to get in trouble or do I not want trouble?" And I decide I don't want to get in trouble, take off my stuff, stand up, go back in and hang my jacket up.

(Reinforcing mindmapping)

C: You were thinking about the consequences. Thinking about, "If I do this, I know what the consequences are—I'll get myself in trouble and it's not worth it."

K: Yeah.

(Mindmapping)

C: How do you make yourself think about the consequences?

K: I just do it.

(Accepting ownership statement)

C: Yeah, but you know something tells me that there are some times that you don't do it and some times that you do it. So there's a difference. And what's real important is that if you know what that difference is, you can do it again.

K: And again, and again, and again!

C: See how important that would be? So how do you do it? How do you make yourself think about it before you do it?

K: I just start thinking about it, about when I get in trouble. And if I do it I'll get a punishment. Sometimes when I'm bored I don't want to get myself in trouble. Then the next day things get messed up, my friends come back early. Oh no, and I'm stuck in the house!

C: So you don't want to disappoint your friends, either?

K: Yeah.

C: And yourself?

K: Yeah, and my mom.

C: So you don't want to disappoint yourself, your friends, or your mom.

K: Yeah. I don't want to disappoint my father either. I feel great when I do those things.

(Increased scale rating question)

C: Excellent. When you are at a 6 what will you be doing then? You're at a 5 right now.

K: Work hard. Work hard at being nice.

(Detailing specific behaviors)

C: So how would you make yourself be nicer? What are you going to have to do?

K: Keep saying, "Don't do it, you'll get in trouble if you do it."

C: Think of the consequences?

K: Yeah.

(Flagging the minefield)

C: What would happen if you were thinking those thoughts and being nice, and one of your buddies, one of your friends, starts being mean. How are you going to keep yourself nice?

K: Don't hang around them.

C: Don't hang around them?

K: Just don't hang around them until they change.

C: That would work?

K: Yeah.

(Concluding the session statement)

C: You know, Kasey, I'm real impressed with all that you have been telling me here. You really know what works for you. You have some really good control when you want to be in charge of yourself. You are really good at that. Is there anything else that I need to ask you before I take a couple of minutes to put my thoughts together so I can write you a note?

K: Not that I know of.

   As part of this practice exercise, now write Kasey a message and compare it to the one I wrote to Kasey that follows.

MESSAGE FOR KASEY

Compliment

> I am amazed with your understanding of what you have to do to avoid messing around and fighting. Calling your buddies by their names, talking to them instead of pushing them around, and playing with them work to keep things peaceful.

You also realize that you would be happier if you were to get up on your own in the morning, say hello to everyone in your family after waking up, help your mom cook dinner, and treat the members of your family like you treat your friends. If you were to do these things you think they would be nicer to you in return.

I am really impressed with your ability to tell yourself to "Be nice and don't hurt anybody" 25 to 50 times in your mind to avoid trouble. Your ability to think about the consequences of doing things that will get you in trouble, like sneaking out of the house, shows that you respect yourself, your mother, your father, and your friends and also says you don't want to disappoint them.

Bridging Statement

Because of your desire to improve your relationships with your friends and your family,

Task

I would like you to notice when you are doing the things to be nice to your family and friends that move you toward a 6.

Appendix B

Solution-Focused Guided Imagery Activity

DIRECTIONS FOR
SOLUTION-FOCUSED GUIDED IMAGERY

Participants in this activity need a 15-page booklet in which to record their responses for each step of the process. Each page of the booklet is half of an 8.5- by 11-inch sheet with directions for that step printed at the top with room to write below it. The pages that contain the steps of the solution-focused guided imagery activity in Appendix B can be enlarged and photocopied to create the booklet.

After each participant receives a booklet, begin by reading these directions aloud.

> Each page of the booklet contains the directions for a particular step in this activity along with room to write down your responses and thoughts. Before I read aloud the directions for each step, I will ask you to close your eyes and visualize the situation I am describing as it pertains to you. Then I will give you a few moments to write down your responses. Please raise your hand when you have finished writing your response to that step so that I will know when to read the directions for the next step.
>
> Before we begin, please note that when I ask you to identify specific things or actions that you would be doing, I would like you to respond in observable and detailed behaviors. That is, rather than saying, "I will be friendly," describe the behaviors you will be demonstrating by being friendly, such as,

"I will be smiling, saying hello, and shaking hands." It is like you are describing what you are doing as if you were watching yourself in a movie. Remember to raise your hand when you have finished writing your responses for that step.

Begin by reading aloud the directions for Step 1 on the first page of the booklet. The score indicated by participants in Step 1 serves as a pretest measure and the score indicated for Step 15 serves as a posttest measure.

Step 1

Close your eyes and picture a recent recurring problem that you would like to overcome. This could be something you would like to do, or something you want to stop doing.

Rate the severity of this problem from 0 (the worst it has ever been) to 10 (nonexistent) and write the rating in the space provided.

My rating is _____

Step 2

Close your eyes. *If your problem is something you would like to do*, picture what it would look like as if it were a video of what you would observe yourself doing behaviorally. Do not describe something you would not be doing. After you have visualized a mental picture of this, write a description of what you pictured in the space provided.

If your problem is something you want to stop doing, picture what you would be starting to do instead. Picture what it would look like as if it were a video of the behaviors you would observe yourself start to do. Do not describe something you would not be doing. After you have visualized a mental picture of this, write a description of what you pictured in the space provided.

_____

_____

_____

_____

_____

Step 3

With your eyes closed, imagine that a miracle happened tonight while you were sleeping, and this miracle solved your problem. Because you were sleeping you didn't know this miracle had occurred. When you woke up you realized that you no longer had this problem. Picture in your mind what would be the first small sign that would show you were doing something different. After you have a mental image of this different behavioral action on your part, write your description of it in the space provided. Do not describe something you would not be doing.

_____

_____

_____

_____

_____

Step 4

With your eyes closed, picture in your mind who would notice this different thing you would be doing and imagine how you think they would respond when they notice this different behavior. After you have a mental picture of this, write your description of what you imagined in the space provided. Do not describe something they would not be doing.

_____

_____

_____

_____

_____

Step 5

Close your eyes and imagine what you would do in reply to the person's response to your new behavior described in the previous step. Then write your description of how you pictured you would respond to that person. Do not describe something you would not be doing.

_____

_____

_____

_____

_____

Step 6

With your eyes closed, picture in your mind who else would notice this different thing you would be doing and imagine how you think they would respond when they notice this different behavior. Then write your description of what you imagined in the space provided. Do not describe something they would not be doing.

_____

_____

_____

_____

_____

Step 7

Close your eyes and imagine what you would do in reply to the person's response to your new behavior described in the previous step. Then write your description of how you pictured you would respond to that person. Do not describe something you would not be doing.

_____

_____

_____

_____

_____

Step 8

With your eyes closed, picture in your mind a time when you've been having this problem yet some of this miracle has already happened, even if only a little bit. Then write your description of what you pictured. Do not describe something you would not be doing.

_____

_____

_____

_____

_____

Step 9

With your eyes closed, picture in your mind how you made this part of your miracle happen during this problem time. It could have been things you thought or tried that were different. Then write your description of how you pictured what you were doing to make some of this miracle happen. Do not describe something you would not be doing.

_____

_____

_____

_____

_____

Step 10

Close your eyes and imagine or remember your thoughts about how pleased you were with your efforts at the time. Then write a description of the thoughts you imagined or remembered. Do not describe something you would not be thinking.

_____

_____

_____

_____

_____

Step 11

With your eyes closed, picture in your mind how you now would rate the severity of this problem from 0 (the worst it has ever been) to 10 (nonexistent) and write the rating in the space provided.

My rating is _____

Step 12

Close your eyes and imagine how you have gotten yourself to that number. Construct a mental image of how you made this happen. Then write your description of what you pictured. Do not describe something you would not be doing.

_____

_____

_____

_____

_____

Step 13

With your eyes closed, picture in your mind when you are one number higher on the scale, what will you and others see you doing that's different from what you have already done? Then write your description of what you pictured. Do not describe something you would not be doing.

_____

_____

_____

_____

_____

Step 14

Write yourself a short note describing what you discovered or rediscovered about yourself and your situation. You can use the back of the sheet if needed.

_____

_____

_____

_____

_____

Step 15

Rate the severity of this problem now that you have gone through this exercise, from 0 (the worst it has ever been) to 10 (nonexistent).

My score is _____

Upon completion of the activity, a group discussion can be held about what students learned from going through the activity. Volunteers can read the short note they wrote in Step 14 and they can talk about how their scores changed and what they will do to continue to improve.

References

Altarriba, J., & Bauer, L. M. (1998). Counseling the Hispanic client: Cuban Americans, Mexican Americans, and Puerto Ricans. *Journal of Counseling and Development, 76*(4), 389–395.

Aviles, R. M. D., Guerrero, M. P., Horwarth, H. B., & Thomas, G. (1999). Perceptions of Chicano/Latino students who have dropped out of school. *Journal of Counseling and Development, 77*(4), 465–473.

Berg, I., & Miller, S. (1992). *Working with the problem drinker.* New York: Norton.

Berg, I. K., & Steiner, T. (2003). *Children's solution work.* New York: Norton.

Biafora, F. A., Jr., Taylor, D. L., Warheit, G. J., Zimmerman, R. S., & Vega, W. A. (1993). Cultural mistrust and racial awareness among ethnically diverse black adolescent boys. *Journal of Black Psychology, 19,* 266–281.

Blackwell, A. (1997). Create-a-puppet. In H. Kaduson & C. Schaefer (Eds.), *101 favorite play therapy techniques* (pp. 194–198). Northvale, NJ: Jason Aronson.

Bruce, M. A. (1995). Brief counseling: An effective model for change. *The School Counselor, 42*(5), 353–364.

Campbell, P. R. (1994). Population projections for states, by age, race, sex, and Hispanic origin: 1993 to 2020. *Current population reports,* Series P25–111. Washington, DC: U.S. Bureau of the Census.

DeJong, P., & Berg, I. K. (1998). *Learner's workbook for interviewing for solutions.* Pacific Grove, CA: Brooks/Cole.

deShazer, S. (1985). *Keys to solution in brief therapy.* New York: Norton.

deShazer, S. (1987, September/October). Minimal elegance. *The Family Therapy Networker, 11*(8), 57–60.

deShazer, S. (1990). *How to establish well-formed goals in solution-focused brief therapy* (The Solution-Focused Brief Therapy Audiotape Series). Milwaukee, WI: Brief Family Therapy Center, P. O. Box 13736.

deShazer, S., & Molnar, A. (1964). Four useful interventions in brief family therapy. *Journal of Marital and Family Therapy, 10*(3), 297–304.

Downing, J., & Harrison, T. (1992). Solutions and school counseling. *The School Counselor, 39*(5), 327–332.

Holcomb-McCoy, C. C. (2001). Exploring the self-perceived multicultural counseling competence of elementary school counselors. *Professional School Counseling, 4(3),* 195–201.

Hosford, R. I., Moss, C. S., & Morrell, G. (1976). The self-as-a-model technique: Helping prison inmates change. In J. D. Krumboltz & C. I. Thoreson (Eds.), *Counseling methods* (pp. 487–495). New York: Holt, Rinehart & Winston.

Kral, R. (1994). *Solution-focused methods for school problems* (A Brief Family Therapy Audiotape). Milwaukee, WI: Brief Family Therapy Center, P. O. Box 13736.

LaFountain, R. M., Garner, N. E., & Eliason, G. T. (1996). Solution-focused counseling groups: A key for school counselors. *The School Counselor, 43*(4), 256–267.

Littrell, J. M., Malia, J. A., Nichols, R., Olsen, J., Nesselhuf, D, & Crandell, P. (1992). Brief counseling: Helping counselors adopt an innovative counseling approach. *The School Counselor, 39*(3), 171–175.

Littrell, J. M., Malia, J. A., & Vanderwood, M. (1995). Single-session brief counseling in a high school. *Journal of Counseling and Development, 73,* 451–458.

Metcalf, L. (1995). *Counseling toward solutions.* Englewood Cliffs, NJ: Center for Applied Research in Education.

Murphy, J. (1994). Working with what works: A solution-focused approach to school behavior problems. *The School Counselor, 42*(1), 59–65.

O'Hanlon, W. H., & Weiner-Davis, M. (1989). *In search of solutions: A new direction in psychotherapy.* New York: Guilford.

Osborn, C. J. (1999). Solution-focused strategies with "involuntary" clients: Practical applications for the school and clinical settings. *Journal of Humanistic Education and Development, 37,* 169–181.

Pelsma, D. M. (2000). School counselors' use of solution-focused questioning to improve teacher work load. *Professional School Counseling, 4*(1), 1–5.

Phelps, R. E., Taylor, J. D., & Gerard, P. A. (2001). Cultural mistrust, ethnic identity, racial identity, and self-esteem among ethnically diverse black university students. *Journal of Counseling and Development, 79(2),* 209–216.

Robinson, T. L., & Ginter, E. J. (Eds.). (1999). Racism healing its effects. [Special Issue]. *Journal of Counseling and Development, 77*(1).

Selekman, M. D. (1997). *Solution-focused therapy with children: Harnessing family strengths for system change.* New York: Guilford.

Sklare, G. B. (2000). Solution-focused brief counseling strategies. In J. Carlson & L. Sperry (Eds.), *Brief therapy with individuals and couples* (pp. 437–468). Phoenix, AZ: Zeig, Tucker & Theisen.

Sklare, G. B., Sabella, R., & Petrosco, J. (2003). A preliminary study of the effects of group solution-focused guided imagery on re-occurring individual problems. *Journal for Specialist in Group Work, 28*(4), 371–381.

Thompson, R., & Littrell, J. M. (1998). Brief counseling for students with learning disabilities. *Professional School Counseling, 2*(1), 60–67.

Walter, J. L., & Peller, J. E. (1992). *Becoming solution-focused in brief therapy.* New York: Brunner/Mazel.

Weiner-Davis, M., deShazer, S., & Gingerich, W. J. (1987). Using pretreatment change to construct a therapeutic solution: A clinical note. *Journal of Marital and Family Therapy, 13*(4), 359–363.

Yalom, I. (1995). *The theory and practice of group psychotherapy.* New York: Basic Books.

Index

**CORWIN
PRESS**

The Corwin Press logo—a raven striding across an open book—represents the union of courage and learning. Corwin Press is committed to improving education for all learners by publishing books and other professional development resources for those serving the field of K–12 education. By providing practical, hands-on materials, Corwin Press continues to carry out the promise of its motto: **"Helping Educators Do Their Work Better."**

The American School Counselor Association (ASCA) is a worldwide nonprofit organization based in Alexandria, Virginia. Founded in 1952, ASCA supports school counselors' efforts to help students focus on academic, personal/social, and career development so they not only achieve success in school but are prepared to lead fulfilling lives as responsible members of society. The association provides professional development, publications and other resources, research, and advocacy to more than 15,000 professional school counselors around the globe.